CALLED TO ACTION

CALLED TO ACTION

Dustin LaChance

Scripture taken from the New King James Version®. Copyright © 1982 by Thomas Nelson. Used by permission. All rights reserved.

Scripture quotations marked (NIV) are taken from the Holy Bible, New International Version®, NIV®. Copyright © 1973, 1978, 1984, 2011 by Biblica, Inc.™ Used by permission of Zondervan. All rights reserved worldwide. www.zondervan.com The "NIV" and "New International Version" are trademarks registered in the United States Patent and Trademark Office by Biblica, Inc.™

Scripture quotations from THE MESSAGE. Copyright © by Eugene H. Peterson 1993, 1994, 1995, 1996, 2000, 2001, 2002. Used by permission of NavPress. All rights reserved. Represented by Tyndale House Publishers, Inc.

ISBN: 1530576970
ISBN 13: 9781530576975
Library of Congress Control Number: 2016904452
CreateSpace Independent Publishing Platform
North Charleston, South Carolina

To my wife, Sara

I love you!

Foreword

When I first met Dustin, he brought renewed hope to my life.

I had just moved to California from Kentucky, and although I loved the weather, there was one thing I was missing: Chick-fil-A. At the time, California had very few of them, and none were within driving distance. That's why I'll never forget the day he walked into our offices at the church to tell me that he had just moved to California and would be opening a Chick-fil-A restaurant right down the street from us. I couldn't contain my enthusiasm; I jumped up and ran over to hug him.

Over the next five years, I got to know Dustin as more than just "the one who brought me Christian chicken;" I got to know him as an entrepreneur and leader. He's always open to what God is doing next and seeking to rise to the challenge. I was also able to know him as a philanthropist. He leveraged his business like his did his personal finances- with great generosity and care. Lastly, I came to know him as a friend. He's one of the most generous and loyal people I know.

When Dustin talks about responding to a call to action from God, it is not the locker room rhetoric that we've all come to know and tune out. It is his own life plan, his own inner dialogue, and, I believe, a message from God to him and through him for all of us to hear. Responding to God's call on his life is not just something that Dustin teaches, but lives.

Dustin's response to God led him to move back to his home state of Florida. He has trusted God through some very trying situations, both personally and professionally, and his faith has become stronger through those difficulties. With the assistance of a stellar team he has helped unleash a movement of compassion and generosity, not just in our community, but across the country, and even worldwide.

I have seen through Dustin's example that when God places a calling on your life, He will relentlessly pursue you. God has challenged Dustin, me, and you to answer a call to action. It's exciting, it's scary, and it's going to be a wild ride! When God directs your life, you are never bored.

I encourage you to pray for fresh eyes and perspective as you read this book and discover what God has planned for you. Be blessed.

Rusty George
Lead Pastor, Real Life Church
Author of *When You / Then God*

Table of Contents

Acknowledgments

I am so incredibly happy that God orchestrated the creation of this book. I am also incredibly happy that it's over! But of course, it's never really over. On to the next one! I would be remiss not to thank some of the most important people in life for helping make the book a reality.

Thanks to my wife, Sara, for all her help in bringing the book to completion.

Thanks to my mother, Kathy, and my brother, Donovan, for the constant support and encouragement.

Thanks to everyone I have ever had the immense pleasure of working alongside at Chick-fil-A.

Thanks to the people I get to serve with at church: Alex, Tim, Jeff, Shannon, Paul, Brandy, KJ, JP, Jim, Rich, and so many more!

Thanks to every member of church! The desire in your hearts to get the lost saved and the saved discipled is changing our community in a BIG way.

Thanks, most importantly, to God. He gave me life and a purpose. He has blessed me with more than I will ever deserve. He is the reason for the hope I have and the unending joy in my heart.

Introduction

Purpose. It's a buzzword these days whose meaning has been diluted and blurred to the level of catchy Facebook banners and running shoe commercials. Is your purpose really to run the four-minute mile? To do the *Thirty-Day Burpee Challenge*? Or maybe get two PhDs? Once you have accomplished any number of these things, will you feel content that you have fulfilled your life's purpose? I would imagine not.

I do believe at some point in time, you have wondered, as we all do, what life is all about. Why are we here? Why do we pursue the things we do? Is it all a huge accident, or is there some sort of legitimate, overarching purpose to it all? There was a time in my life when I was plagued by these questions. I would ask those questions but had no idea what the answers were, and when this problem arose, it usually resulted in a feeling of hopelessness and helplessness. I believe this question haunts many of us, regardless of our varying stations in life. It afflicts the young, the poor, the old, the middle-aged, the rich. The question usually becomes more difficult to ignore as we get older and we begin to ponder our legacy. Is it all for nothing? Or are you like me? Do you have the persistent sense there must be something more for you than the life you currently live?

I once read a story about an accomplished businessman who saved a large company from bankruptcy. Years later, after his numerous significant achievements, he reflected on his life and came to the conclusion that he desperately needed to write a book. In his book, he shared his deep, dark secret that despite his many successes and vast wealth, he still desperately questioned the meaning of life. He had aggressively and passionately pursued fame, fortune, and power and had achieved what he had set his heart on. Only in reaching his goals, however, had he realized none of it gave him meaning or purpose. The ultimate question still eluded him.

I don't know about you, but I certainly don't want to come to that realization at the end of my life. How crushing would it be to feel the years you have been given were wasted? This question so gnawed at my soul that I reached the point where I could not spend one more day questioning my existence. It was only when I was ready to receive the truth—whatever that might be—that some truly remarkable things began happening. But please be aware there was undoubtedly a different path I could have chosen. If you don't remember anything else from this introduction, please remember this: if I had walked this alternate path, I would have sacrificed truth for my own pride and rejected an answer that jarred my skewed existential framework. Although it was a tough pill to swallow, that path would have led me in circles, chasing one fleeting illusion after another. If you choose that path, you will likely become frustrated and depressed and continue living a life of mediocrity, desperation, and hopelessness. The second option is much, much brighter. It takes courage, however. You have to have reached a point where you are willing to hear what God has in store for you *personally*. And you need to *act* upon it.

I sure don't claim to have all the answers, but I can show you what I've learned firsthand and do my best to lead you to the One who does have all the answers. These questions and feelings of loneliness and emptiness are unnecessary and ironically, the answer has been in front of you all along. The key to unlocking it is to simply have a willing and trusting heart. Please don't think for a second I am promising a quick and easy solution. You're smarter than that. Difficult questions will be posed. Some you may initially scoff at, and some may make you pretty angry. That is because these uncomfortable questions and ideas require *change*, and change requires *movement*. Movement is often difficult. Although I will ask you some tough questions, you have my word that I have asked them of myself. And I have personally moved through these questions to a fulfilling place where I know the answers without a shadow of doubt. These chapters will be provocative, but if you take the time to diligently explore your mind and heart, I will go so far as to promise you will find what you have been searching for. The choice to change, however, rests squarely upon you alone. The first step of the journey is up to you. The second will come more easily.

You may wonder: *Is he going to preach? Is he going to jam God down my throat?* Yes and no. I'd be lying if I said my life hasn't been entirely revolutionized, and I'd be lying despicably if I said God wasn't the catalyst for that change. So yes, I'm going to talk about God, but no...I'm not going to force Him on you. I find it helpful in my own life to consider, at times like these, I have a preconceived notion of God based on my life experiences. Some of that perception may be accurate, but I know it is mostly inaccurate. This is why we need open hearts to comprehend who He truly is and why He loves us *personally*.

As I share stories from my personal life, you'll soon see I have not always had such peace and fulfillment. I, too, struggled with the question of my existence. As a young man, I was taught the stories of the Bible, and I believed in God, but I knew very little of whom God is. I called myself a Christian because I went to church and occasionally gave of my time. I hung out with the "right people," I didn't do drugs, and I was mostly kind to others. Overall, I thought I was a good person, but I knew my perspective was skewed because I was still unfulfilled. I continued in that direction for years until I found a girlfriend, thinking I would find the fulfillment I was craving in marriage. That was when God began to change my heart. For many years, I had read the Bible sporadically without obtaining much value or change. Then, I started to make a point of daily reading, comprehension, and practical application. The scriptures I read sparked something inside my heart to the point where I knew, at the very least, there was undoubtedly a sure answer to the meaning of life. I wasn't yet sure of what God's plan was for me, but I had entered into a purposeful and fulfilling relationship with Him unlike anything I had experienced before. I found real joy. You can find it too.

It can be discouraging to think of how far we have drifted from the creatures God destined us to be. We have all undoubtedly missed opportunities that would have fulfilled us in a way nothing on this earth ever could. But we needn't be sad. Although we may have missed out on past things God has planned for us, the story does not end there. It may seem impossible to recover what we've lost, but Jesus said, "With man this is impossible, but with God all things are possible." Friend, there is hope, and there is still a magnificent future for those who believe. God is patiently waiting for us to turn to Him and to respond to His call. We only need to trust and believe. That's great news!

As you've probably guessed, I have written this book for those wandering through life without meaning or purpose, just as I was. This book is written for those who truly yearn for a more meaningful life. I pray that after you have read this book, you will know your search for purpose and fulfillment is over. I pray you will be willing to surrender yourself completely to God's purposes and in your surrender, He will be able to bring you the pleasure of a meaningful life, both now and in eternity. I also pray this book inspires you to read and study the Bible with the rest of your time on earth, so that you may develop a lasting relationship with God.

This book is divided into three segments:

The first section, *A Wake-Up Call*, is written to awaken your mind to the true fulfillment you are missing in life and the magnitude of what could be yours. God does not call us because He's bored. He desires our success and has greater purposes for us than we could even dream for ourselves.

The second section, *Take Action*, is written to carry you to the depth of your motives and honestly analyze them. Once you surface, you will realize there are changes that need to be made. These changes may be difficult at first, but the journey to fulfillment will become easier as you progress. The key to refocusing is building a consistent relationship with God.

The last section is titled *Finding Your Purpose*. Now that you have awoken and refocused your life, discovering your individual, God-given purpose on earth is just an arm's length away. Discover what it really means to become a disciple of Jesus Christ and become a shining light and example of fulfillment to the world. Yours will become a life that is instantly noticed and desired by others. You will have a life filled with God's joy and peace. It will be the fulfilled life you can never receive from this world.

So what are you waiting for? It's time to stop making excuses and start making some positive changes. Some things may be difficult to hear, but change is not supposed to be comfortable or easy. Only you can decide to respond to what you read. It is your choice to adjust how you live each day, and it is also your choice if you remain unchanged and continue living how you have been. But I encourage you to turn the page and start your journey toward the fulfilled life you've only dreamed of.

Section 1

A Wake-Up Call

In this first section, my primary motivation is to expose you to ideas either you may not have been considering or you may be ignoring. These ideas revolve around the common themes of the book, which are taking action regarding your walk with God and taking steps toward your ultimate calling of sharing the gospel of Jesus Christ. This section, however, is designed to awaken your mind to all that you are missing in life and what you could have if you were to wholeheartedly pursue God's calling.

God didn't call you because He has nothing better to do; He has a great and powerful purpose for you, and He wants to use you! In this section, I will also begin to show you how to take those first steps to realize and understand your calling. As you'll see, much of my personal testimony includes refocusing my life away from material pursuits, despite God blessing me in the area of business. As such, I'll be talking a lot about living the life of a giver and examining what our primary focus is.

The bottom line of this section is that God loves us and is actively wooing us to do more so we can be truly blessed in this life and after. We just need to be willing to hear His voice and answer His call.

Let's get started.

1

The Gift

Envision for a moment that I'm holding a bomb. The bomb has a large, red LED display, and the seconds are ticking down. 1:21…1:20…1:19…I am standing in front of you in a locked, underground bunker. It doesn't really matter how we got there. What matters is how we get out. *If* we get out. What would go through your head? What questions would you ask? What actions might you take? 1:15…1:14…1:13…I know what I'd be thinking. *We need to figure out how to disarm this thing before it kills us!* So which wire do we cut? Green? Black? Red? Would it even help, as the movies portray, or would it cause the bomb to instantly detonate? I think it's safe to say we'd both be pretty afraid. Would we try to run? Maybe place the bomb in one corner of the room and cower in the other? Or would we just let the time run out in denial because we don't know how to save ourselves?

If, in fact, we were locked in a bunker together with a ticking bomb, would we panic as we tried to figure out how to

prolong our lives? Or would we be comforted in the knowledge of what will happen when we die? Would our lives have
meaning? If we had certain answers to those questions, would
we even feel safe taking a chance and cutting the red wire,
just to see what happens? Here's the cold truth: Our lives *are*
ticking time bombs. They will end. What happens next? As we
begin this journey together, I want to ask you to not only consider that question for yourself, but perhaps more importantly,
to also consider it for your loved ones.

Hopefully, this is not a situation any of us will ever encounter, but I present this scenario as a metaphor for life. My life is
going to end, and your life is going to end. The days, hours,
and minutes of our lives tick away like a timer on a bomb.
The truth is, you cannot disarm this bomb, and the clock is
undoubtedly running down, whether we want it to or not. The
scary thing, however, shouldn't be how or when we are going
to die. Instead, it should be what choices we have made before we *inevitably* do.

Now, imagine Jesus approached you with a priceless gift,
and instead of gratefully receiving it, you turned and ran as if
your life depended on it. Why would you run? Let's think about
it...have you ever run from a relationship with a crazy ex, a
job you hated, or even circumstances you couldn't tolerate?
Maybe you ran away from home or moved across the country
because you couldn't deal with your situation anymore. Things
like this happen all the time, but can you imagine running

away from a gift? The only explanation I can think of is that you somehow had no idea it was a gift.

One of my favorite stories in the Bible is the story of Jonah. The Lord comes to Jonah and essentially says, "Up on your feet, boy!" I love that! I can imagine Jonah's reaction as God prompts him to stand up and get ready. Jonah knew these archenemies of Israel were sinning horrifically and in time, God could no longer ignore their transgressions. As an upstanding Israelite, Jonah was looking forward to the day when God would judge Nineveh, and at first it appeared as if that wonderful day had come...but God did something unexpected. He told Jonah to go and preach to the Ninevites, giving them an opportunity to repent and be saved from their sins and ultimate judgment. The Lord was offering them a way out, and something inside Jonah told him the Ninevites might seize the opportunity.

Rather than obeying God, Jonah made a different choice. He ran in the exact opposite direction of Nineveh. He very deliberately went to the docks, found a ship, paid his fare, and told the crew to get him as far away as possible. While they sailed, a huge storm arose. The waves began crashing against the bow, and water began to flood the decks. The ship started threatening to break apart in the monstrous waves, so the crew began throwing their cargo overboard. When that didn't work, the sailors, huddled together, wondered why they were facing such unusual danger. They cried out for salvation to their respective gods, but only Jonah knew exactly why the storm was afflicting them. In denial, he didn't share his knowledge with anyone. This sounds familiar, doesn't it? When something cataclysmic is happening in our lives, observers watch and wonder, but deep down, we know the reason for our trials. We know the truth. We know we have gotten ourselves into a bad situation because we are intentionally outside of and running from God's will.

You know what Jonah did instead of seeking the Lord? He went below deck and fell asleep. When the crewmen couldn't find him, one of them went below deck and, yelling, gave Jonah a rude awakening, crying that he should be praying to his God instead. You can imagine that Jonah wasn't happy being awoken, but it brought him squarely into the reality that he and the crew were going to die if he slept through the storm. Even the ungodly crew knew this storm was unusual, and they understood their very lives depended on figuring out the cause. They decided to draw straws to find out who was responsible for their plight. Predictably, Jonah drew the shortest straw.

The crew immediately insisted he tell them what he had done to cause the catastrophic storm. When he'd boarded the ship, they only cared that he could pay his way. Now, they demanded to know where he was from, what he did for a living, where he was going, and what he had for breakfast. Jonah answered, "I am a Hebrew, and I worship the Lord, the God of heaven, who made the sea and the dry land." The sailors grew frustrated and asked again what he had done to cause the storm. As Jonah explained himself, he eventually realized he was running from God. Recognizing that if the storm continued, the ship would be destroyed and they would all die, Jonah knew his situation was dire and only extreme measures would save the ship. Jonah told the crew to throw him overboard. His redeeming quality was acknowledging he'd made a mistake by running from God, and his weakness was risking other people's lives.

The crew, however, displayed more concern for their fellow man than Jonah originally had. They refused to throw Jonah overboard. What a lesson for Jonah. Something tells me he initially regarded the righteousness of these sailors rather lowly, but here they were, insisting on attempting to row back to shore, being willing to risk their own lives to save Jonah's. Eventually, Jonah convinced them he was absolutely to blame for his choices, and seeing that everyone was going to die regardless, they relented, cried out to God for mercy, and threw Jonah overboard. Immediately, the storm subsided.

In awe, the crewmen worshiped God. Although Jonah had been running, God used the situation for His glory, saving the souls of these men unfortunate enough to cross the path of a man called of God but in denial (or outright rebellion). God revealed Himself to the crew and saved them in the process, but God was not done with Jonah yet. Jonah 1:17 says,

> Now the Lord provided a huge fish to swallow Jonah, and Jonah was in the belly of the fish three days and three nights. (NIV)

When I heard this story as a child, I absolutely did not believe it. How could it be true that a fish (or whale) swallowed a man whole and that he survived three days inside it? I used to think this story was crazy, but now I think differently. Archeologists have discovered fossil evidence of *huge*, extinct fish that could very well have accommodated such a feat. We don't know how recently these fish became extinct, so in my humble opinion, Jonah's story teaches us that if God wants to get your attention, He can and will use any means necessary. God will pursue you to the ends of the earth and will never quit. How you respond, however, determines the length and intensity of your journey.

"Why would He pursue me so relentlessly?" you might ask. Great question. Perhaps you may not know you're running from a *gift*. A gift that He knows will change your life. Something you may have no idea is going to bring you ultimate purpose and meaning and, more importantly, to change others' lives.

While in the fish's belly, Jonah prayed:

> In trouble, deep trouble, I prayed to God. He answered me. From the belly of the grave, I cried,

"Help!" You heard my cry. You threw me into ocean's depths, into a watery grave, with ocean waves, ocean breakers crashing over me. I said, "I've been thrown away, thrown out, out of your sight. I'll never again lay eyes on your Holy Temple." Ocean gripped me by the throat. The ancient Abyss grabbed me and held tight. My head was all tangled in seaweed at the bottom of the sea where the mountains take root. I was as far down as a body can go, and the gates were slamming shut behind me forever—yet you pulled me up from that grave alive, O God, my God! When my life was slipping away, I remembered God, and my prayer got through to you, made it all the way to your Holy Temple. Those who worship hollow gods, god-frauds, walk away from their only true love. But I'm worshiping you, God, calling out in thanksgiving! And I'll do what I promised I'd do! Salvation belongs to God! Jonah 2:2–9 (The Message)

Then, God spoke to the fish, and it regurgitated Jonah onto the shore. Why did it take such a dramatic series of events for Jonah to turn back to obeying God? Later on in the story, we see some hints. Believe it or not, Jonah hadn't fully learned the lesson of love and concern for others' eternal future. He went and preached in Nineveh, and the city repented, even wearing sackcloth and ashes to show their remorse. Jonah's old way of self-righteousness cropped up, as we see in the following passage:

But to Jonah this seemed very wrong, and he became angry. He prayed to the Lord, "Isn't this what I said, Lord, when I was still at home? That is what I tried to forestall by fleeing to Tarshish. I knew that you are a gracious and compassionate God, slow to anger and abounding in love, a God who relents from sending calamity. Now, Lord, take away my life, for it is better for me to die than to live."

But the Lord replied, "Is it right for you to be angry?" (Jonah 4:1–4) (NIV)

It would be heartwarming to know that Jonah eventually relented and understood that these Ninevites were simply lost, but that's not what happened. Jonah found a great spot, overlooking the city, to watch the lightning and fire fall from the sky in judgment on the great city. God sent a couple more trials his way, trying to wake Jonah again to the fact that we're all sinners and God loves us all equally. And the only reason he was called as a preacher was because he simply obeyed God's will in the past. And the book of Jonah *ends there*. We never know if Jonah overcame his anger and resentment of the Ninevites. Jonah had plenty of self-justification for hating Nineveh. It was the capital city of Assyria, a nation that had brutally plagued Israel for hundreds of years, with a particular reputation for violent crimes. It didn't matter to God. When they responded, He forgave them. I believe God wanted Jonah to be the picture of forgiveness and love, the foreshadowing of Jesus in this capacity. God had a tremendous gift for Jonah, and while I believe he still received a good portion of it, he definitely missed out on a good portion. Jonah simply wouldn't listen, or he would have understood God's loving ways.

So where are you in your journey? I promised I would ask the tough questions, and here are a few. Your life is ticking away. Are you sleeping through it? Is a storm raging around you, and deep down, you know how to stop it? Are you maybe in the belly of a fish, at your rock bottom, your breaking point...is this attempted wake-up call your last chance?

You may be running from Jesus in any number of areas in your life, and He may have had to take drastic measures to get your attention. I know people who had to lose everything before they opened their hearts to God. Why do some of us have to lose it all, often more than once, before we wake up and acknowledge the storm? When will we say, "Enough is enough! I will trust God is good with every fiber of my being!" If you think you're okay, consider your actions may inadvertently be hurting others. If God is calling you to do something, but you are afraid and choose to run, what effect will this have on the people around you? Whether you are the leader of your family or business or the lowest man or woman on the totem pole, people are taking note of your life. Do they see a fulfilled life, lived to serve Jesus? If your actions aren't helping others, could they be wreaking havoc while you nap?

Jesus is undoubtedly calling out to you, but perhaps you feel you aren't ready. What are you afraid of? Are you running? Hiding in the corner while the bomb counts down? What would happen if you gave your life completely to Him? I can guarantee there will be change. Big change. It will be scary at times, and you will have to rely on your faith, but I will also guarantee your life will be better than you ever could have dreamed. And consider for a moment that Jesus is pursuing you with a *gift*. It's a gift greater than anything you can imagine, but you're afraid to open it and look inside.

2

Growth and the Power of Choice

If your family is anything like mine, you probably go out to eat every so often. When we go out, the first and possibly the greatest family challenge we face is where to go eat. I'll be honest—the discussion about where to eat frequently devolves into an argument. We all have different tastes, so we each suggest a place and try to see if a majority emerges. That rarely happens. I like to eat at places like Chipotle or Subway because I can choose exactly what I want. My wife usually picks Mexican or Greek restaurants. Now, I love Mexican and Greek cuisine, but at a full-service restaurant, you can't always customize your meal to get exactly what you want. This is why I am such a huge fan of Chipotle (man, I *love* Chipotle!). I can create exactly what I like on my oversized burrito (for the record: steak, black beans, hot sauce, corn salsa, and extra sour cream) and get out the door for around seven dollars. If I try to order *moussaka* at the Greek restaurant with extra rice and garlic but with zucchini instead of eggplant, I'm liable to cause some serious plate smashing in the kitchen. (I'm kidding! Sort of.) Living in the modern world affords us many choices and opportunities, and not just regarding food. We choose where to seek higher education, what career to pursue, what kind of car to drive, and more. Every day, we're making choices. What's interesting is that choice often brings with it a dilemma. In his book *The Paradox of Choice: Why More Is Less*, author Barry Schwartz presents some compelling research that argues too many choices actually make us unhappy. Hmm.

To add to our personal choices, as we get older, we often have to make choices on behalf of others. Our children are an obvious example: we decide what school they'll go to, how to help them through a crisis, or when to tell them *No*. Eventually, though, we all grow up and have to make decisions for ourselves. In fact, one of the amazing things about God is that He gave us the freedom of choice. We aren't marionettes on strings, without control over our lives. No, we're individuals—unique, weird, and wonderful. The freedom of choice, of course, produces some interesting (and often amusing) results. Have you ever seen someone and questioned why he or she chose a particular car, haircut, or denim pantsuit? I have to admit, people watching is one of my favorite pastimes. It may sound like something the elderly do at the mall, but it can be really eye opening. As I watch people, I often think:

"Is that dude really wearing a mesh top?"

"Oh my gosh, someone needs to tell her she tucked her shirt into her underwear."

"There is no way plaid shoes go with a polka dot shirt."

"Why does that woman have a ferret on a leash? At the mall?"

Although I can be catty at times, I think it's wonderful that we each have individual personalities and can express ourselves however we choose. God created us that way, and I believe He gets great joy out of watching how we choose. God created us to make our own choices, but I know without a doubt He also wants us to make the *correct* choices (more on that later).

When going a little deeper in discussing choice, it only makes sense to go back to the beginning. Let's consider Adam and Eve; have you ever wondered why God put the tree of the knowledge of good and evil in the Garden of Eden? If the tree hadn't been there, there would have been no sin. There would be no crime, no rape or murder, no cancer, diabetes, pain, or suffering. The human race would be completely different. I have talked with several people over the years who've questioned God's decision to place the tree in the Garden. They usually haven't considered, however, that without the tree, we wouldn't have the freedom of choice. Essentially, we wouldn't necessarily be robots, but we would have been sheltered from the reality of choice. We'd simply be following God without any conscious love or intention. Would you want to be unknowingly sheltered, your strengths and victories hollow? Would you enjoy being someone who doesn't have the freedom to make decisions on your own? When God said He created us in His image, that includes possessing the freedom of choice. Some may say Eve made the choice to sin and then Adam followed. Although that is technically correct, it is not the point here. God *had* to put the tree in the garden because He is not a tyrant. He wanted us to *choose* to trust His direction rather than be forced to obey Him. What some view as inexplicable on God's part is actually one of His greatest gifts to us: the power of choice.

Of course, our relationship with God doesn't end in the garden of Eden. Any power carries with it a burden of consequence. The power of choice is no different. Especially when it comes to relationships. Choosing where to go out to eat or whether to buy a new pair of pants is one thing, but choices in our relationships are where the rubber really meets the road. I like to think of these simpler choices as training wheels for the weightier choices: things like choosing to love and honor my wife or choosing to follow and obey God. Relationships are also where we see a deeper reflection of consequence. I absolutely have the power to choose to put my selfish needs first, but with that choice comes the *burden of consequence*.

"So what about God?" you may ask. "Sometimes it feels like He is just pulling strings, and we have to make all these tough choices while He gets to judge them?" Oh, friend, God has chosen to make the biggest sacrifice of all. God entirely put His heart out there and laid it all on the line for us. When it comes to relationships, no one has made more sacrificial choices than God. Time and again, He has done this, the most significant of which was sending His only begotten Son, Jesus Christ, to be tortured and die in our place and for our selfish choices. No one tops God when it comes to good choices. The irony, of course, is we still have the choice to accept His sacrificial gift or spurn it.

I never want to come across as conceited but honestly, in one way, I sort of understand how God may feel about us at times. I pursued my beautiful wife, Sara, for many years. I waited patiently for the day she would choose me and finally say, "Dustin, I'll be your girlfriend, your wife. I love you!" I put myself out there so many times, hoping and praying I would be Sara's choice. Unlike God, however, I was obnoxious at times, pushing the issue and even trying to force the relationship. I was ready, but I was trying to force a choice from her. God never does that. I wanted so badly for her to tell me she loved me too and was ready for a relationship. In the end, however, it had to be her decision. If it weren't, I would always have lived with the nagging feeling she was bullied into marrying me.

As I waited for Sara to respond with an open heart, God is waiting for us to respond in the same way. He has opened the door for a relationship, just as I did with Sara, but the choice must be made by the pursued, not the pursuer. Sara had to decide whether to choose me as her partner, and we have to decide whether or not to choose God. But you know, the real question is, *Why wouldn't we?* God is good. He is a good father. He is a source of comfort, a guide for the future, and an ever-present source of help in times of trouble. I believe the only reason we *don't* choose God is that we are misinformed on many levels. I believe this misinformation, or *deception*, is related to the burden of consequence. God only wants to bless us and to tell us great and unsearchable things that we don't yet know. He wants us to live the full lives that He has intended. The relationship, however, is dependent on my choice, your choice. We literally have the power to enter into a relationship with the Creator of the universe at any time, but we clearly don't because we are misinformed. You have many choices to make, but believe me when I say the only one that truly matters is whether you will choose God. He has already chosen you, no matter how sinful, how dirty, or how lost you may be. But please believe He has already chosen you.

For a moment, let's step back to the idea of consequence. If you buy a car and realize you really don't like it, you can trade it in for another. Yeah, you'll lose a bit of money on the taxes and maybe a little on the markup price, but it's not the end of the world if you made a bad initial decision. Alternately, you might go to a restaurant and take a chance ordering an entrée that turns out to be not to your taste at all. No problem—you can usually send it back and choose something else. Those are small choices, but they do carry a degree of preparation for larger choices. Many of the choices and decisions we make each day aren't as life altering as we'd like to think; however, there are some that are critical. At some point in your life, especially if you live in the Western world, you will be presented with the choice to begin a relationship with Jesus Christ. This is a choice that will change everything for you. Please bear with me and allow me to change the tone for a moment. You see, this choice will affect not only this life but the one to come as well. If you don't believe there is a life after this one, respectfully my friend, you have been *severely* misinformed. What's more, your choices regarding the information you are reading right now could affect where you will spend eternity. God wants you in His life; do you want Him in yours? I have never met a single person who said, "You know what? That whole 'giving my life to Christ thing' was a huge mistake. I am much happier without Him." That simply does *not* happen.

Now, you may be asking the common question, "If God loves us so much, how can He send someone to hell?" That's a fair question, and you have every right to ask it. Let me ask you—if you are a parent, do you do your very best to guide your children in the right direction? You might pay for private school and even college tuition. You might not allow them to date until they are older, or you might not let them watch certain movies in your house. In the end, however, it is ultimately their choice to listen to you and obey. If they really want to run wild and rebel, they can. You may have raised them correctly since birth, put them in Sunday school, and forbidden them to date anyone who doesn't share your values, but children will still make their own choices because they are human. You cannot force them.

You see, because God gave us the power of choice, we each have a mind of our own. We are equipped with the choice of free will. If you are asking the question, "If God loves us so much, how can He send someone to hell?" respectfully, again, you are misinformed. God doesn't send us to hell. Hell is the only destination available for those who *choose* to separate themselves from God for eternity. You see, God gives us the power of choice but even goes a step further. He tells us what choice is best. In Deuteronomy 30:19–20, God tells His children:

> This day I call the heavens and the earth as witnesses against you that I have set before you life and death, blessings and curses. Now choose life, so that you and your children may live and that you may love the Lord your God, listen to his voice, and hold fast to him. For the Lord is your life, and he will give you many years in the land he swore to give to your fathers, Abraham, Isaac, and Jacob.

From this scripture, we can plainly see God deeply desires for us for make the right choice so He can subsequently bless us. He has placed the choice between heaven and hell squarely into our hands. Is there really a question about where we want to spend eternity? Of course not! Heaven, obviously!

I don't want to choose hell; I can't imagine how terrifying it must be with all the beings who choose to separate themselves from God's love and goodness. If you're misinformed, however, you could believe that God is waiting to send you there because He's angry with you. But you're no longer misinformed; you are awakening from that sleep we mentioned in the previous chapter.

If my choices are to submit to a loving yet absolutely almighty God as He generously directs my path or try to figure out if there is anything outside of the Creator in this life, I think the choice is a no-brainer. Again, this is the single most significant choice you will ever make. God does not want anyone to be separated from Him, but just as we saw Adam and Eve do it in the garden, without provocation from God, we can choose it ourselves. Unfortunately, just as with all other facets of life, there is the reality of the burden of consequence, should we reject God. Jesus Christ, God in the flesh, died for us. If we reject His costly, ultimate sacrifice, there is nothing more God can do for us. In fact, and these are my own words, there is nothing more God *should* do for us. We are choosing not to submit to His Godhood, something akin to a private in the army spitting in the face of the general of the armed forces. In fact, that's a crude metaphor; God ranks infinitely higher than a general. He loves us so much, however, that He continues to pursue us despite our stumbling away from Him. As long as we have breath in our lungs, God extends the choice to love Him back.

Shifting gears for a second, let's look at the situation as it stands in reality for many of us. Spiritually speaking, we see there is a progression here. We have to choose God initially, and this begins our faith walk. But what then? Actually, before we can walk, we have to begin crawling. This ties in to the freedom of choice because very few people can consistently make the right choices, day in and day out. That requires an advanced level of spiritual maturity, which, like anything else in life, requires *practice*. If we're honest, even after we have surrendered to God, have accepted His precious Son Jesus, and are enjoying the liberating joy He brings, we frequently stumble and fall in our dedication to Him. It's a constant cycle, isn't it? We take a step forward, face a new challenge, usually stumble, and come back to Christ, walk in His mercy, and then we fall again. I do believe, however, that we can avoid this pattern for the most part. In the Apostle Paul's second letter to the Corinthians, he says something very interesting:

> And we all, who with unveiled faces contemplate
> the Lord's glory, are being transformed into his image
> with ever-increasing glory, which comes from the Lord,
> who is the Spirit. (2 Corinthians 3:18)

Some translations say, "…transformed into His image from glory to glory." This tells me that we don't have to take a step back each time, and I believe the key is in that same verse. We need to be transformed into *His image*. I believe this comes back to being conscious of our choices. Once we've taken the first step in surrendering to God, if we keep focusing on Christ, we'll take the correct steps (choices) in faith after that. This is where we learn to crawl and then learn to walk. I believe a big part of it is learning to lay down our selfish decisions and instead turn to God for guidance.

So we've accepted Jesus as our Lord and given our daily life to Him, and we're feeling pretty good. Now what? Do we try to get rich? Do we try to move to a neighborhood where there are more "good" people and live conservatively? Do we try to shun those people who are still misinformed (deceived) so they don't contaminate us as we try to be transformed into Jesus's image? Of course not. That might make sense according to the world's logic, but not according to God's logic. Remember, you are saved by grace and through faith, so guess how you'll continue growing? Yep! By grace and through faith.

I see so often, however, that we simply choose to do nothing about the lost's lack of knowledge of God's love. We watch apathetically as our friends, family members, and coworkers stumble in the dark, live in fear, and deal with problems they could easily overcome with Christ. Yet we often feel afraid or even unqualified to share the ultimate hope that we have. Why is that? We see people daily who live without Jesus, but we do absolutely nothing about it. We assume they will come to Christ someday, but we somehow think it will magically happen without our intervention. This, my friends, is another choice. We can see now how the choices keep coming, even after we're saved. The good news is that as you embrace them and choose to make the right decisions, you move from glory to glory. In this way, we see the focus of our choices shift as we mature. The focus moves from ourselves to others. As God pursued us, so we begin to pursue others. This is how God intends us to live and grow.

As you probably have guessed, I haven't used the example of sharing Christ with others by accident. After our decision to follow Christ, this choice is the single most important one of our Christian walk. Think about it. Someone was courageous and sacrificial enough to share the gospel with you, why shouldn't you do the same? If it's made all the difference for you, why wouldn't it for that person you know you should share the gospel with? Honestly, how would you feel if someone's time ran out? What if someone you knew was never invited to church or never experienced Jesus's love, and it could have made all the difference? Perhaps your attitude and faith have intrigued a friend of yours, and perhaps Jesus is tugging at his or her heart, while you are choosing to ignore the prompting to invite her or him to church. You keep putting it off until tomorrow, but you must remember that we are not guaranteed a tomorrow. I urge you to make the conscious choice to take action now because you never know what tomorrow holds.

Once you have committed to the idea, you will quickly realize how many opportunities we have each day to speak with others about God. Look around you right now. You may be at work, in a coffee shop, or sitting at home across from your unsaved spouse. There is probably someone nearby who doesn't know Jesus. You can make the choice to seize the opportunity and not give up. After all, it's *eternal* life we're talking about. If you are rebuffed, keep trying. I understand, on the other side of the coin, some situations exist where perhaps you have been reaching out to the same friends or family members for eons and they have yet to make a change. You may be tired of trying to teach them about Jesus and share the hope you have, but their ears and hearts aren't ready to receive the information. You feel frustrated, and you may even give up. I encourage you not to. Even if they aren't ready yet, those seeds are being planted and watered. They will sprout eventually.

In my life, I have known many non-Christians who needed the Lord, but in the past, I assumed that they would find Him on their own eventually or that someone else would step up to the plate. I never really thought of it as a pressing issue. I think I secretly feared pushing the topic and making them angry. Then I realized I was being a coward and admitting that I didn't value them enough to talk to them about God. That's a hard realization when it comes. If you won't share your faith with others, do you really believe in eternal life and eternal death? It's a tough question, but in the spirit of crawling before we walk, let's examine our reasons for not sharing Jesus with others. Some of us feel uncomfortable or shy, and others just don't have enough faith in themselves (or God) to begin the conversation. I know I personally didn't tell some of my friends about God because I didn't think they would change. I had no faith. This was when I realized that if I believe someone I love is too far gone to be rescued by Jesus, I had a harsh truth to face: I was the one who didn't have enough faith in God. I'll tell you straight: God put that person in your life for a reason, and He is able to accomplish more than we could ever imagine. You may worry that if you put yourself out there and share your love for Jesus, others may judge you or even end their relationship with you. The truth is that how others respond is not your responsibility. All you can control is what you say and how you act.

So lastly, as we begin to crawl and make the choice to bring up our faith with those around us, we'll begin to understand that our responsibility even goes beyond simply sharing the gospel with people; we must also consider the examples we set each day. I love a quote that is often ascribed to Francis of Assisi: "Preach the gospel at all times. Use words if you must."

Here's the reason why we must live the gospel, and not just talk it: I have encountered several people that just weren't ready to hear the gospel. As I developed as a believer, I began to realize that instead of trying to force-feed these people the Word, my job instead was to be a good example and *demonstrate* the truth in love. A great example I can use is a man very close to me, whom I care about dearly. I will keep his identity anonymous for various reasons, but I assure you he is a real person. Recently, I was talking to—let's call him Jim—on the phone. He is not even sixty years old but is in very poor health and has been near death for years. Although doctors are continuously surprised he is still alive, it is no surprise to me. God has a purpose for Jim! For so many years, however, his heart was deeply hardened toward God. He had absolutely zero interest in hearing about God or Christianity from me or from any of his family or friends.

During one of our conversations, Jim was complaining about his life. He said he wished so much that he could go back in time and make different choices. Jim can barely walk up a flight of stairs without nitroglycerin, he can't see very well, and he has a very difficult life in general. One day, he finally admitted to me that if he had made better choices as a young man and, most importantly, accepted Jesus into his heart, he would have a completely different life now. I was astounded and overjoyed to hear this confession. After so many years of decrying Christianity, Jim had a change of heart—an epiphany, at the age of fifty-nine.

What came next, however, shocked me. After his revelation, Jim asked, "Dustin, why didn't you ever tell me about Jesus?" As I reeled, I tried to figure out the best way to explain that several of his family and friends had tried to tell him about Jesus more times than I could count. Jim simply had not been ready and hadn't had open ears. I explained that although we had shared Christ with him, rather than continually beat him with a Bible, we had tried to also demonstrate the love of Christ and be living examples of our Lord. We didn't stop speaking with him about God; instead, we wanted him to see the difference in our lives. Did we ever fail in our example? Of course, many times! Still, we prayed for grace and never gave up the hope that Jim would come to know the Lord. And he did!

You see, Jim was not raised in a Christian home. A relationship with God was not even once a topic of conversation. His family didn't attend church and never truly heard about the hope that Jesus brings. Jim's mom was an alcoholic who sold herself to men to provide for her children. Throughout his childhood, Jim called three different men "dad." At one point, two of them even lived in his home at the same time. Jim simply did not have a sound upbringing, and he definitely was not set up for success. When Jim was little, for some reason, his mother decided that he and his brother were going to live on the porch of their trailer home. When it rained, as it inevitably does in Florida, they would get soaking wet, and they couldn't do anything about it. So guess what Jim did when he grew up? He hoarded worldly possessions so he would never experience the lack he'd had as a child. Can we blame him? Of course not! It's a sinful, fallen world we live in, and the reality is there are cases much, much sadder than Jim's within arm's reach of each of us right now. Finally, however, at almost sixty years old, from a continual example coupled with Biblical wisdom, Jim realized that worldly possessions would never fill the void in his heart. He finally admitted only Jesus Christ could. Jim now understands that material possessions grow old, break, rust, and eventually vanish.

Believe me when I say it took a lot for Jim to become a Christian. He had to be truly humbled before he turned to God. Prior to accepting Christ, he went from being pretty well off to having absolutely *nothing*. He lost his money, his job, his savings, and even his relationships. Jim reached a point where he had no hope. In fact, all he had left was his wife and sadly, it took losing her too to make him finally realize he needed some divine assistance. That sounds very familiar, doesn't it? Either we are the same as Jim, or we know someone is in that boat. Why do we so often have to hit bottom before we realize we need Christ? Why does something horrific or life changing have to happen in order for us to see that our lives are pointless without God? I know everyone has his or her individual challenges, and some have been through some difficult experiences, but I wish so much that the world would understand if we started living for Christ now, everything would change for us. The good news is that we have that choice!

Sadly, Jim understands—probably better than most of us—the burden of consequence. Even though Jim has staked his claim on eternal life, he often expresses his wish to rewind the hands of time and redo countless events. I can't imagine being sixty years old and having a lifetime of regrets. God can redeem the time, but it would be so much easier for Jim if he had only made the right choices as a younger man. Perhaps someone close to him made the fateful choice not to share the gospel with him. Someone he would have listened to. We will never know what Jim's life might have looked like if he had accepted Jesus in his younger days. Thankfully, Jim has finally accepted Christ. He also realized that while it is not always a bad thing to want a nice car or a beautiful home, the ultimate desire of his heart should lie in Christ alone. This may seem like an easy concept to grasp for most of us, but Jim has only recently understood that this life is temporary and that nothing the world can give us will last through eternity. James 4:14 says,

> Yet you do not know what your life will be like tomorrow. You are just a vapor that appears for a little while and then vanishes away.

This life means nothing without a relationship with Christ, and I can't express how huge a blessing it is that Jim has become a Christian. I pray that his path will give you hope if you know someone who still isn't ready to hear about God. Never, ever give up on someone! It may get tough, even after someone comes to the Lord, but stick with it. That is going from glory to glory! You're sitting up, and then you're crawling, and next you'll be walking, and then running at full speed. It's tough for me to admit, but I'll openly say that sometimes I find myself reverting to silently doubting Jim. He's not perfect and still has a lot to learn. I watch him sometimes and think to myself, *I just don't see it. It's hard to believe that your conversion is genuine. I don't know how long this change is going to last.* Then, I force myself to take a step back and reevaluate. *Who do I think I am? It's not my job to determine if Christ has really changed his heart. Only God knows that, and only God needs to know.* My job is to support him as a fellow Christian and encourage him when the walk is difficult. This too is living as an example of Christ.

Jim is making some radical changes now that he is a Christian, and I know it will not always be smooth sailing. He has six decades of bad habits to change. He will fall flat on his face at times, just like the rest of us. He may be tempted to fall back into his old routines and bad attitudes at times, but that is Jim's process of crawling and then walking. At the very least, he now realizes there are better options for his life. The beautiful part is watching this unfold in someone else's life, knowing you had a part to play in his or her progress. This *really* bolsters one's own faith.

Perhaps you're in Jim's situation, though. As you hear his story, you may be thinking it isn't applicable to your life. Your situation may not be as extreme as Jim's, and you may not have lost everything, but perhaps you are in the midst of a tough situation and are determined to manage it on your own. Maybe you haven't reached out to God for help because you think you are strong enough to handle your own problems. Friend, allow me to be the first to pop your bubble. You can do *nothing* without God's help. If you just rely on God and ask

Him for help, your life will change. I promise it. I guarantee it. At first, it may be a small change, several changes, or maybe even a huge change, but you won't know until you surrender to Christ. Stop trying to do it all on your own; you aren't meant to.

As we venture into the following chapters, I'm sure you can feel something awakening inside you. I pray you continue this journey with me with an open heart. There is so much more good stuff to get into. We'll discover together what it means to have a true purpose and calling from God. I encourage you to open yourself to discover why God gave you breath, because He is ready to use you in ways that will fulfill your wildest dreams, if you are ready to trust in Him.

3

Birds of a Feather

So far, we've looked at what the most critical and effective choices for our lives would be, both now and in the future, and how from there, we should take gradual, baby steps to a mature faith. I also told you about Jim, who had wasted much of his life making the wrong choices but ultimately made the right one. Jim was blind to the spiritual realities that were affecting his life, but eventually he made it. Now, it's very easy to use Jim as an example and say, "Boy I'm glad that isn't me," or "Man, how could he be so stubborn?" In my opinion, every single person on earth today has not fulfilled the call of Jesus on their life, and it's likely very few are walking in the perfect will of Jesus. I understand that is a bold statement, but walk with me through this chapter, and you may agree. You see, we're going to take a closer look at a few things that may, unknown to us, be causing "blind spots" in our lives. These blind spots can derail your spiritual future if you ignore them.

When I was a kid, my dad always said, "Birds of a feather flock together." It didn't always make sense to me at the time, but now I completely understand. We, as human beings, tend to surround ourselves with people that are most like us. In fact, I believe we actually seek to hang out with people and then slowly become like them. You see, we choose the people we allow into our daily life based on mutual interests or pursuits, and whether we like it or not, we are undoubtedly influenced by others. I understand some of you may see yourself as strong willed or as a leader, rather than a follower, but the truth is that we each follow something. We choose our friends for a reason: we enjoy their company, we have similar personalities, they do things we enjoy doing. Yet it is important to note that we find ourselves emulating one another. I don't believe there is anything inherently wrong with that, but can it be a bad thing?

When I was a teenager, I loved Eminem. Adults warned me I should never listen to his music because it would corrupt my heart, but despite his lyrics being filled with profanity, violence, and domestic abuse, I disagreed. When I was older, I was determined to watch R-rated movies. A movie earns that rating because it contains violence, nudity, drug use, profanity, and an assortment of other elements that are unsuitable for children. Adults insisted these movies would corrupt my mind too, but I insisted on watching them. In time, it became easier for me to listen to more explicit music. Then it was easier for me to watch more explicit movies. I started off with nothing too rough, a mere swear word here and there, and then watched movies with unmarried couples in bed together, and then I was allowing all sorts of explicit, sexually sinful situations, violence, hatred, murder, and more into my mind. I watched it under the guise of "suspended reality" and entertainment, but I began to emulate the behavior, and it almost pulled me away from my Savior and cost me everything I'd worked for.

Now, I understand there are many out there who perhaps weren't as sheltered as I was and grew up in much harsher circumstances. This gradual drawing into sin might seem like child's play to you, and perhaps it was. Sure, some of us were smoking marijuana at ten years old and had our first sexual experiences before we were teenagers. That's just the reality of the world today, but even in those circumstances, it began somewhere, with someone abandoning Jesus's principles in our lives.

The point I'm making is that sin always begins insidiously. Something as seemingly harmless as music can subtly introduce ungodly thoughts, attitudes, and even aspirations into your life. Think about popular music today; I don't think you can disagree that flagrantly casual sex, alcohol and drug abuse, and self-centered rebellion are the *de facto* topics. And never mind the underground, hardcore stuff; that's just the popular, mainstream music!

You see, many times in the Bible, Jesus or the disciples in their later years called believers *children*. The way we're created is to emulate what we see. Our children emulate our behavior. Orphans emulate their caretakers in the orphanage. Children emulate each other at school. If we allow ourselves to be exposed to negative influences, no matter how subtle or seemingly benign, it's the slippery slope that blindsides us.

How easy is it for our choices to become a slow, downhill progression? You open the door with a casual flirt with the cute new hire at work. He or she responds, and suddenly you feel a rush. You know you'll never let it go anywhere, but the excitement, the rush, and the attention are addictive. "It's a bit of harmless fun," you tell yourself, but you know you'd never act that way in front of your spouse. Suddenly, there's a secret between you and your spouse, and one day, the two of you have a huge fight. You suddenly realize you're feeling neglected, and to make it a perfect storm, you're asked to work late on a project with your flirty colleague. What's next? If you don't do something drastic to eject from the situation, suddenly you've transformed into an unrecognizable version of yourself.

I understand some readers may disagree and even feel a little defensive. You may point out that there's nothing wrong with looking at a woman in a bikini or at the *Sports Illustrated* swimsuit issue, especially if you're a single guy. "That's how Jesus made us, right? We can look, as long as we don't touch!" I contend, however, that the women in those pictures are someone's daughters or someone's sisters, and they all have souls. I can also guarantee you're not thinking about their personalities or assessing if they're the perfect model of a Proverbs 31 wife as you flip through the pages. Please hear me. I'm not saying this to place restrictions on you. I'm simply pointing out you have a skilled, cunning enemy who will use anything possible to slowly—preferably blindly—drag you into hell with him. Something seemingly innocuous as the swimsuit issue can lead you down the slippery slope to pornography. Once you get there, it's far easier to rationalize adultery; your brain will have already been programmed toward that end. Friend, believe it. I have watched it happen.

Here's a question you can ask yourself up front: "How far am I willing to go?" Before taking that prescription pain pill "just to unwind," ask yourself, "Will it really just be this one time?" Maybe you're justifying a gambling addiction with your analytical personality. Sure, you just enjoy a few hands of blackjack, but how far are you willing to go? Will it stop with just a few hands? What if you lose money? Are you going to try to get back to breaking even?

Or maybe your addiction is food. Yes, the sin of gluttony (Proverbs 23:20–21) is an epidemic in America today, and I've found that *especially in churches*, this one is glossed over. I'm not judging anyone, but are you really going to get into shape and take care of your body this year? Our bodies are the temple of the Holy Spirit. Where do you see yourself in a year? How is it affecting your health? Maybe your temptation is the opposite: you're addicted to the gym. Or you're addicted to your Instagram and Facebook accounts. You friend every "hot" girl or guy you talk to, and you leave flirty, sexualized comments on Saturday night and then hit up the eleven o'clock service on Sunday.

Again, please understand I am not judging. I struggle with the same temptations; that's why I know to ask, "Where will I draw the line?" At some point, you will have to draw a line, but you may find yourself in catastrophe before you reach that line if you don't remain vigilant. You can go nowhere near that slippery slope, and you must make the decision to stop now.

What if we had a perfect blueprint that we could overlay onto our lives and use to figure out exactly what would be best for us, both in the short term and in the long run? I'll admit, working for something feels good. When I resist that flirty glance from the Starbucks barista or say no to a night out with the "old crew" when I know they're going to be getting into shady stuff, it feels great! At first, it may be tough, but the next day, you feel a sense of accomplishment.

Why wouldn't that apply to your entire life? Here's an often-overlooked secret: we fool ourselves into compromising because we say we don't want to become *extremists*. "I don't want to be one of those girls who doesn't know how to have fun. It's just one more drink!" Or "I don't want to be one of those religious nuts who doesn't do anything fun." Don't fool yourself. There is more joy and power in serving Jesus than you could ever imagine.

I think it's no secret that Hollywood, corporate America, and the world at large are all trying to sell you something. Do you honestly believe they care about how their products and sales strategies affect you? They don't even know you, and believe me, you don't really know them. (I'd take a wild guess and say your average entertainment exec probably doesn't hit up your Bible study on a Wednesday night.) Yet we emulate what we see from them, every day. The marketing ingenuity of Madison Avenue proved this resoundingly in the early part of the twentieth century, and the advertising industry is a *lot* more savvy and powerful today. It is well known that early advertising pioneers consulted with psychologists to subliminally influence people to purchase their products. What basic human motivations do you think they focused on? It was sex, prestige, and power, all focusing on the *self*. Not very Christlike traits, wouldn't you agree? The bottom line is this: If you don't set boundaries for yourself, who will? (Answer: No one.)

I know this is an uncomfortable chapter, but I also have to say something because if I don't, someone else may not. And this is a critical step toward finding and fulfilling your purpose in Christ. I'm certainly not saying you can't flirt with people other than your spouse, go to drunken parties on Friday nights, or pop painkillers just for fun. I'm just saying it's a bad idea and asking you to not deceive yourself about how it starts. Most importantly, however, I'm cautioning you about the consequences. Jesus gave us the gift of free will, and we all have to make choices that are right for ourselves and our families. It boils down to how you want to spend not only your life but eternity. I'm also not saying that if you know Christ and you sin, you will not go to heaven. Yes, Jesus absolutely loves you and will forgive your sins if you ask, but more than that, He wants you to obey Him and return His love. Why? *Because you'll begin to emulate Him!*

If you were in a human relationship where you only received love but never reciprocated, I guarantee it wouldn't last long. Unfortunately, our relationship with Christ is all too often one-sided like that. We simply take Him for granted. He gives us gifts, blessings, protection, love, and comfort. We gladly accept what He offers and then forget to give back. All Jesus asks in return is that we love and obey Him, but it is impossible to do that if we allow things that dishonor Him to corrupt our lives. When you choose to watch a movie that grieves your spirit (and the Holy Spirit within you) or listen to explicit music, you are putting those things above Jesus. The Old Testament symbolism of *idols* is what these things become. An idol is anything that takes Jesus's place. Anything that supersedes obedience to what you know will please Him. It's easy to see that this world and everything in it is deteriorating fast, no matter how flashy and attractive it seems at times. Isn't it therefore entirely foolish to waste our time on choices that don't glorify Jesus?

Okay, I want to discuss a (true) Bible story in light of our look at unknown hindrances to our faith or our "blind spots." Most of us know the story of Sodom and Gomorrah, and we associate those cities with sexual depravity and ultimate judgment. There is a lot more to that story, though. Sodom and Gomorrah were two cities that were rich agriculturally and cultivated a lot of fruit, especially. They were good at it, and their commerce was highly desired. There is at least one account of rich trade between Syria and Sodom. My point is this: Sodom and Gomorrah were very attractive cities, according the standards of this world. Their citizens were liberal, rich, and by all accounts lived how they wanted to and were seemingly successful in their pursuits. Sound familiar?

> Abram lived in the land of Canaan, while Lot lived among the cities of the plain and pitched his tents near Sodom. (Genesis 13:12)

The scripture above takes place after Abraham and Lot (his nephew) needed to split up because their individual prosperity had grown too great for single pieces of land to feed both of their animal herds. Even though traveling with Abraham was the entire reason Lot was so blessed, Abraham gave him the first choice of what land he would like to take. Lot chose the greenest, choicest land that also happened to be pretty much right next to Sodom. Lot knew and understood who God was, and he had to know the spiritual depravity of Sodom, but in the scripture, he made his home next to Sodom anyway.

> Then Abram moved his tent, and went and dwelt by the terebinth trees of Mamre, which are in Hebron, and built an altar there to the Lord. (Genesis 13:18)

In contrast, in the scripture above, we see Abraham went west, far away from the sinful cities, even thought that land was not nearly as rich and lush. But Abraham was thankful and honored the Lord by building an altar there regardless. Predictably, despite making his home, with all his herds and tents and servants (all blessings from God) in time, overlooking the city of Sodom was not enough for Lot. He must have developed relationships by trading some cattle for fruit and vegetables. His servants must have made friends with the Sodomites. Slowly, it only made sense for Lot to move his home into the city. Yes, before long, Lot went from walking with the father of faith to living in Sodom, surrounded by total depravity.

Make no mistake, Lot was a respectable man with good morals. He, however, was deceived in thinking he could live in a city saturated with sin and remain unscathed. Lot didn't draw the line right in the beginning by honoring his uncle, even seeking his advice and allowing him to choose the good land. Lot *desired* to live near Sodom. It was a big, rich, happening city, and this probably excited Lot to a certain degree. With that small, initial step, corruption was inevitable not only for Lot but for his family.

After Lot moved into Sodom, Abraham was approached by the three "angels" (or messengers) of God (one of whom was Jesus). Jesus told Abraham He was going to destroy Sodom and Gomorrah because the outcry of these cities had long risen up to him. Abraham was rightly concerned because his nephew, Lot, was living inside the city. Abraham asked if the Lord would destroy the righteous with the wicked, and reasoned, "What if you found fifty righteous? Would you still destroy the city?" Jesus replied if He found fifty righteous people living there, He would not destroy Sodom. Abraham was much bolder than I would have been, and the Lord would spare the city for forty-five people. Jesus agreed, so Abraham pushed his luck. He bargained with Jesus: forty, thirty-five, thirty, twenty, ten. "What if only ten righteous can be found there?" Abraham pleaded. Jesus agreed again not to destroy the city for only *ten* righteous people out of an entire city. What an astoundingly generous God! (Do you see how valuable your righteousness is, not only to yourself but also to the unsaved around you?) God was gracious enough to spare a rather large city for the sake of a measly handful of righteous people. When I first read this story, I thought, *God has some serious anger if He's willing to destroy an entire city*. But now I see the truth: God loves us! He would have saved the entire, extremely wicked city for only ten righteous. But you know what? Not even ten could be found.

Abraham presumed ten was a safe number, since Lot had family there as well, and surely Abraham could count on them to be righteous? Alas, only one righteous person was found in the entire city of Sodom. At this discovery, two angels took human form and entered the city. Lot greeted them and invited them into his house, knowing it was not safe for them to stay in the city square. Sodom was so wicked that the townspeople started to bang on Lot's door, demanding he open it so they could have sex with the strangers who had just arrived. As they tried to break down the door, Lot begged the people to leave the strangers alone, trying to appeal to their long-lost sense of morality. Then, Lot did something unthinkable: he told them that instead of the strangers, the townspeople could have his two virgin daughters. The city was so sinful and Lot had become so corrupt that he was willing to sacrifice his daughters.

Even Lot's sons-in-law who had married into his family thought he was joking when he tried to warn them. God waited for Lot to escape and then righteously destroyed Sodom and Gomorrah. As they reached the city of Zoar, which Lot had negotiated for God to spare, Lot's wife sadly disobeyed their angel escorts and looked back as the cities were destroyed. In doing so, she revealed her bond with and longing for the sinful cities and turned to a pillar of salt. (Yes, I believe that actually happened.) Through one corrupt decision years earlier, Lot reached a point where he lost just about *everything*.

> Then Lot went up out of Zoar and dwelt in the mountains, and his two daughters were with him; for he was afraid to dwell in Zoar. And he and his two daughters dwelt in a cave. (Genesis 19:30)

Lot was lured in by the flash and attraction of the city of Sodom. He ignored his heart's prompting and ignored what he knew was the right thing to do. You see, God will never allow the wicked to flourish forever. Evil simply doesn't last. If we immerse ourselves in the world, even casually at first, before we know it, we will lose everything. Sodom became Lot's focus until it became his desire; he watched the people and saw what they did. Pretty soon, his family (at the very least) were emulating the sinful Sodomites. In the same way, when we watch certain movies, listen to certain music, or surround ourselves with people who dishonor God, we take a step further away from Him. We move our home closer to Sodom each time we think about these things. Before long, we're living in the city.

I hope I have proven how corruption sneaks into our lives in small ways. If you allow it in, it will undoubtedly take over your whole being before you realize it. Even if you just compromise a little, *you will have to make twice as many tough decisions just to get back to where you were.* You may have the knowledge to do right, but the things and people that you surround yourself with can make you forget very quickly. James 3:11 says, "Can both fresh water and salt water flow from the same spring?" Pay careful attention to where you pitch your tent.

Take some time to examine your life. Maybe your tent is pitched toward that dream car, a trip to Vegas, or maybe even an attractive, married coworker? Vegas isn't all bad (they do have some amazing churches), but when you visit, what are your plans and intentions? God knows what is in your heart and mind. It's difficult to go to Las Vegas and be a believer, just as it is difficult to go to certain parties or hang out with certain friends and be a believer. Are you pitching your tent near something that is displeasing to God? Remember, you are not a bird of the world's feather. Don't try to be like them. You are light, and they don't know why, but they really want what you have. Don't believe otherwise. You have a responsibility to show them the way, not to allow them to corrupt you so they feel less guilty about their sin. That is why *compromise is sin*.

I urge you to run from it. You needn't lose all your friends, stop watching movies, stop listening to music, or become a boring, sad person. On the contrary, you will become a leader, a trendsetter, someone people know as having a backbone. Yes, it will be tough at times, especially finding the balance of your heart's conviction, but you and God will decide together what is acceptable. When God destroyed Sodom and Gomorrah, He gave Lot and his family the chance to run away. His only requirement was that they flee the city and never look back. There is a lesson there. It's good advice for all of us. *Flee from sin!* Don't look back! Your old life, those old friends, and that old attitude have nothing for you. You can't keep living in sin and claim to obey God. You have to run at full speed from it; you must be willing to obey God at any cost.

The best part is this: When you run from sin, at the same time, you are clearing the obstacles from your path. You are placing mirrors in your blind spots. Once you begin walking in your faith, unhindered, whew…that's when some power starts to flow. That's when the miraculous starts happening. You become focused, life becomes rewarding, and *your divine purpose begins to become clear.*

4

Jim's Left Leg

Many of the threats to fulfilling your ultimate purpose are pretty evident, and some are not as apparent. In the last chapter, we discussed how small compromises can subtly derail your calling over time, but there exists a cousin to compromise that can be far more insidious. Like compromise, this threat does not manifest as a sudden, severe abandoning of one's faith, yet in time, it can have the same lethal result. That is your enemy's objective, and he's in it for the long haul. You really are in it for the long haul too (whether you like it or not), yet this hindrance can keep you in a downward-spiraling trap of mediocrity, causing you to think that someday you may begin to take steps toward complete devotion to God. For some reason or another, though, today never becomes that day. I'm talking about stubbornness.

Do you remember my friend, Jim? I'm going to tell you more about his backstory. I told you he made wrong choices and ultimately lost everything (just like Lot), but despite Jim's macho exterior, he wasn't completely ignorant of Jesus's calling. True, Jim was never much of a believer, but in times of trouble, he would cry out to God. Jim knew he should be serving God, but he never did, and as a result, his life was quite a roller coaster. That is until one day, being particularly down on his luck (at least he believed it was luck, not poor choices), Jim became so depressed he contemplated suicide. It was at this point, I suppose, Jim's stubbornness caved in, and he probably reasoned that finally giving in to Jesus was better than dying. Instead of taking his life, Jim went to church.

He took his Bible and drove to a little chapel that was open all day for anyone to come in and pray and read in silence. In that little church, in his hour of desperation, Jim poured his heart out to God and laid these troubles before his Creator. Jim was on the right track, yet inevitably, he reached a point where the Holy Spirit spoke to his heart, and Jim knew he would have to completely submit to Jesus. I believe he sensed it couldn't be a one-time thing; it would have to be a daily walk.

This acknowledgement is the first step in truly growing in Christ. The key is to go to your proverbial "chapel" every day and keep building your relationship with God. Without that consistent relationship, your spirit doesn't have the power to override your flesh (your carnal mind and worldly desires). Basically, you can't think straight without the help of the Holy Spirit, and the best to way to energize your spirit is through prayer and studying the word of God. Although I believe Jim sensed this, he still didn't understand the concept of submission to Jesus. I think in his mind, he had a picture of a boring, lame life surrounded by old-fashioned pipe organs and stodgy recitals of archaic Bible stories. Up to this point, Jim had no idea of the ultimately fulfilling, custom-tailored life God had planned for him. He'd been stubbornly refusing to listen because of his preconceived notions. Still, on that day, he had broken down and was talking to God. Jim, however, sought a shortcut out of his problems. He basically wanted a solution, not the Provider of solutions. There is a big difference.

Jim, being a notoriously "independent" guy, decided he was owed something in return for his allegiance to Jesus. He proposed a deal to God, saying, "Lord, if you take care of my money problems and give me a break, I promise you I will honor You and show You glory for what you've done for me." Jim made a vow. It was a reasonable proposal, I guess, although unfortunately, Jim didn't stop there. (When Jim was seven years old, he was diagnosed with type 1 diabetes, so maybe that was where he got the notion of losing a limb, as diabetics have a higher chance of losing a limb than a normal person does). In his prayer, Jim promised that if God bailed him out, and he did not keep his end of the deal and give the glory to God, God could take his left leg. Now why he would promise such a thing is beyond me, but that's exactly what he did.

> When you make a vow to the Lord your God, you shall not delay to pay it; for the Lord your God will surely require it of you, and it would be sin to you. But if you abstain from vowing, it shall not be sin to you. (Deuteronomy 23:21–22)

Jim had reached a point where he put his situation into God's hands, but as he had been casual in his attitude toward Jesus most of his life, he was casual in his attitude toward Him. (I doubt Jim would have allowed a bank to claim his left leg as collateral for a loan to bail him out of his problems.) Jim was a frequent gambler, and that day, as he left the chapel, he looked up at a reproduction of *The Last Supper* by Leonardo da Vinci, and he read a verse beneath it. He opened his Bible to that verse and read it, and somehow the chapter and verse seemed like a sign for numbers he should play in the lottery. I don't know why or how it happened, and I'm absolutely not saying if you make a deal with God, He will give you whatever you ask for, including winning lottery numbers. I'm also going to deal more later with making deals with God, or what He calls *vows*, but for now, please don't misunderstand me. I don't know whether it was God, but believe it or not, Jim won. It wasn't a jackpot, and it wasn't enough money to set him up for life, but it was a significant win nonetheless. Sadly, Jim collected his winnings and was relieved and on top of the world. He was free and clear of his financial problems, but when a prompting in his heart came to follow through on his end of the bargain and give God glory for what He'd done,

Jim ignored it. Soon after, he bought a big home on a mountain in North Carolina and moved his family there. Jim paid off his bills, began prospering again, and still refused to give God the glory. After a while, he just sort of forgot about his promise and went on with life.

One day, Jim and his family went to play at a nearby park. He wasn't usually very playful, but that day, he picked his wife up while pretending to tightrope walk on one of the wooden balance beams. The beam was a little wet, and Jim slipped, fell, and shattered the tibia and fibula in his left leg. It was nothing more than an accident, but Jim ended up staying in the hospital for *over a year*. It was a severe break for such a minor accident, and the ensuing medical issues were even worse. Jim, however, stubbornly refused to acknowledge his betrayal of the promise to God. He subsequently developed osteomyelitis, and in time lost so much weight that at one point he weighed only eighty pounds.

For the longest time, Jim's family truly believed he wouldn't make it. Did God cause Jim to fall off that beam? I don't believe God teaches like that; however, God may have allowed it to wake Jim up. Jim had made a promise to God, and our enemy Satan and the entire spiritual world heard him too. I believe the lesson Jim was failing to see was that he had trusted in a quick bailout. We're always going to face problems, as Jim found out. The lesson was to follow through on our commitments to Jesus, no matter what—not just when we're in dire straits. I believe Jim would have been more prosperous than he could have dreamed if he had only submitted to God and was consistent with his promises.

While in the hospital, Jim had his blood tested every week to monitor the progression of the osteomyelitis. Week after week, his condition worsened until the doctors told him it was terminal and that he should begin making funeral preparations and make peace with his fate. Jim always had to hit rock bottom. I don't know what went through Jim's head. I have my doubts he confessed his sins or asked God for forgiveness, but I do believe when he heard that news, Jim asked God for another chance. When the next blood test was run, there was no trace of osteomyelitis in his body. *None!* Jim was supposed to die but was suddenly healed completely from the osteomyelitis. It was nothing short of a medically documented miracle. Jim soon regained his strength and weight and went home to his family.

After that scare, Jim went home and, as soon as he was healthy enough, went looking for churches to attend. Jim again was on the right track, yet as was his *modus operandi*, he always seemed to stubbornly hold something back. It always had to be Jim's way. Instead of looking for a church that had strong teaching and opportunities for fellowship, Jim chose his church purely because he liked the exterior stonework and the "great view." Jim wasn't building a relationship with Jesus out of trust and love; he was trying to stave off the perceived claim of a creditor. Pretty soon, hard times arose again, and Jim went back to his old mind-set and began living as he had before. You see, Jim had no foundation. Was God really interested in the glory Jim was supposed to give Him? Of course not. He cared about Jim's *heart and motivation*. He cared about what would benefit Jim and knew that was merely the total surrendering point for him. Jim knew he would have to publicly proclaim faith in Jesus, and that meant making a commitment to Him. But as is His nature, Jesus was still astoundingly patient with Jim.

Ten years later, Jim still hadn't kept any of the promises he'd made to God and was living as an everyday sinner in the world. One day, he was walking down the street and stubbed the big toe on his left foot. This shouldn't have been a big deal, but the health of diabetics can be very delicate. When Jim stubbed his toe, it was pushed back right into his foot. After a few days of agony, he had to go to the hospital. After the examination, the news was shocking. The doctor told him that the osteomyelitis had returned and was infecting his entire body. The toe would have to be amputated. Jim ripped out his IVs and literally ran out of the hospital, vowing never to return. You may see a pattern here, and you'd be right. Years earlier, Jim renewed his commitment to attending church and tried to appease God. God had been extremely merciful and patient but was slowly reaching the point where He had to get Jim's attention. Jim, however, was sadly proving to still be too stubborn to hear.

Jim continued living his life as he saw fit, for several years, and either ignored the effects of the blood poisoning or somehow lived with the pain. One day, however, Jim was driving his scooter through the parking lot behind his house. A semi-truck suddenly sped around the corner, startling him, and Jim crashed his scooter. Since it was right behind his house, Jim's family heard the noise and rushed out to help him. Jim lay on the ground in agony, holding his badly injured left leg. The ambulance quickly arrived and took him to hospital. The doctors examined him and gave Jim a grave choice—he could die, or they could amputate his left leg. Jim had been stubbornly ignoring the voice of the Holy Spirit to come to terms with his vows for twenty years. Finally, it had caught up with him. For some reason, Jim had opened the spiritual door to use his left leg as a bargaining chip and discouragingly had not followed through on his end of the bargain. Jim's left leg was amputated.

As you know, the loss of Jim's leg unfortunately didn't wake him up. Rather than something finally clicking in his head (or heart), Jim became bitter and angry toward God. He felt like his manhood, mobility, and ability to provide for his family had been purposely removed. Amazingly, he didn't realize that time after time, God had saved his life for a greater purpose. At the end of the day, although God is staggeringly merciful, He is almighty and an all-powerful God; He doesn't need to be tested by the people He created. How many times have you sent up a prayer like this: "God, just let me win the lottery! I'll never ask for anything again!" or "God, bring me the spouse of my dreams! I won't bother you again if you give me this one thing!" How many times have you bargained with the Savior of the world? I'm ashamed to say that I still sometimes catch myself doing this. I imagine God looks at us and thinks, "I have given you everything you need. Wake up! I have already taken care of you. Have I not brought you this far? Don't bargain with me. I want a relationship with you. That's why I gave my Son for you!" Still, we stubbornly persist in our own will and want more.

I think at the end of the day, it comes back to the deceptive idea that materialism is security. We run toward newer, bigger, shinier, more expensive things to make us "happy." We need to win the lottery to be happy. We need to keep up with the Joneses to be happy. What happens when we die? Can we take with us any of our worldly possessions we so desperately needed? At times, when I'm pondering this topic, I often think about my ancestors. Do I care what mode of transportation they had? Their social standing? What clothes they wore, how lavish their homes were, or if they owned the latest gadget? Of course not. So isn't it funny those worries occupy so much of our time now? We fixate on trivial things that don't truly make our lives easier and will vanish one day. It is highly unlikely the items we are accumulating now will ever make it into a museum. Our cars will end up in scrap heaps, and our homes will be torn down. Nothing material will forever remain of the lives we are living right now. The only investment that can and will last is the legacy of the work we've done for God.

We give far too much focus to this life and not enough for the one to come. That's where Jim lost track. His focus was this life, never giving thought or care to the next. He had many opportunities and heard the truth many times, yet he remained stubborn, even in the little decisions toward God. He missed the opportunity of spiritual blessings. Yes, he won the lottery, something that many of us have prayed or wished for, but so many years later, what did he have to show for it? Absolutely nothing. Christ is knocking at your door, but He will not force His way in if He is not welcome. Ensure that your heart is open and willing to invite Him in. By doing so, you will receive more blessings than the lottery could ever promise.

To end on a light note, the following story portrays what I see as the root of our stubbornness toward God. I once heard a story about a man who was working on a new high-rise in Manhattan. The team was behind schedule due to inclement weather, so they were working late into the night to get caught up. This man was very high up on the scaffolding, and there was little to protect him. He felt the winds whipping about him, and it was so dark he could barely see what he was doing. He worked in minimal light until he was exhausted, and when he thought it couldn't get any worse, a light rain began. He carefully moved up and down a few levels of scaffolding to various locations and worked and worked. All around him were the loud noises you'd expect to hear on a construction site: the hammering of nails, the clanging of metal, the whine of a buzz saw. As he tiredly moved around the scaffolding in the dark, he suddenly made a misstep, lost his footing, and began to fall. In terror, the man grabbed the ledge of the scaffolding with his hand, but in the rain, his grip was slipping. He screamed desperately for help, yet no one could hear him over the noise of the buzz saw, hammering, and rain. Slowly, his grip loosened more and more, until it gave way, and the man fell. He screamed again and knew he would become another job site statistic. A thousand thoughts raced through his head at once: his wife, his children, his family. Unexpectedly, he only fell five feet. There was scaffolding beneath him the entire time that he couldn't see, and he landed with no injuries at all.

Do you sometimes feel like you are barely hanging on, trying to bargain with God for help, yet often not even receiving an answer? Do you stumble through life in the dark, feeling completely alone and helpless, until you reach a point where you're about to let go? Then perhaps you plead with Jesus for relief, answers, and rescue. Have you ever stopped to think His mercy is the scaffolding beneath your feet to catch you? He already has it under control; we just never humble ourselves and give it entirely over to Him. We don't consistently build a relationship with Him where we'll come to know without a shadow of doubt that a platform is beneath our feet. If we can let go of our fears, our hurts, and our hang-ups, He won't actually let us fall at all. If we call to our Creator, He will hear us. He will provide the scaffolding. He will rescue us. We just have to trust.

There is a secret, however, that results in a humble, practically automatic trust in God. I began to understand this secret after a pretty terrifying encounter one night as a teenager. Let's just say I was a victim of mistaken identity, and the realities of hell were suddenly in my face, clawing and tearing at me, dragging me away. I've never forgotten it, and if you keep reading, I don't think you will either.

5

Judgment House

I didn't grow up in a united Christian home. What I mean is that my mom knew the Lord and was devoted to Him, but she was, sadly, living in what we'd call an "unequally yoked" marriage. Picture a team of oxen pulling a plow. One is weaker and distracted. It greatly reduces the other's performance. My dad wasn't a Christian. He had his moments, but for the most part he gave my mom a pretty hard time about it. As a result, I was sort of on the fence about church (that was largely my definition of God and Christianity as a youth). I didn't even attend church on a weekly basis, and I don't think I ever went to Sunday school. When I was about ten or eleven years old, however, a local church hosted this event called Judgment House around Halloween, and it sure sounded a lot cooler than the typical youth group meetings.

Judgment House was predictably marketed as a "Christian haunted house." Basically, the church put on a play that followed the lives of two people who die, one going to heaven, the other to hell. The story began with a couple on their way to prom and their journey through the night's events. The journey started in one room and then moved on to the next as each different scene revealed more of the story. In the first room, our chaperone through the "scenes" asked that all audience members remove their hats. I was a pretty defiant kid and also had an embarrassing bowl haircut, so I ignored the request and left my hat on. *That's so old school, removing your hat in church*, I thought. *Besides, it's not like it's a service or anything.* Since the play was live, we were also instructed to remain behind a tape barrier so as not to interfere with the drama.

In the story, the couple were involved in a car accident on their way to prom. One of the victims died immediately and went to judgment, and the other died later at the hospital. Now I have to say here that the production value was incredible, so as a ten-year-old child, I found it pretty real. We followed the teens to judgment, where we were presented with a door to hell and a door to heaven. As I looked at the doors, I became frightened. I watched anxiously as the young couple was beckoned into the hall of judgment to learn their fate. One, predictably, was a Christian and was welcomed into exhilarating glory. The other was not a believer, and to my horror, was sentenced to depart from God to reside in hell.

We were guided into the next room, where terrible sounds and smells hit us like a wall before we even entered the room, and chills ran down my spine. Then we entered hell. There

was loud, thumping music, and the sounds of people screaming in pain. Somehow, they had managed to make the room
smell like sulfur. As we walked in, I saw people shackled behind a chain link fence and demons leaping about, cackling
and screaming as they tormented them. Behind them, on a
great, infernal throne, overseeing the tortures, sat Satan himself. My blood ran cold, and I will never forget that image as
long as I live. A few younger girls in the group started crying,
and their older sisters or their moms tried to comfort them as
best as possible. But the music kept thumping, the people
kept screaming, and the sulfur kept burning.

Of course, I had to be the tough guy, so I acted as if it
didn't faze me at all. I walked right up to the chain link fence
and placed my face against it and stared at Satan. I felt cool
for a moment. What I didn't realize, however, was that the boy
who had died in the wreck had snuck out back and was now
hiding in our group, wearing a hat. To add to the already high
shock value, the demons were about break through the chain
link fence and pull this guy out of our group. Guess how they
knew whom to pick out? The guy wearing the hat, of course.
Guess who was standing right in front, also wearing a hat?
Assuming I was the actor, the demons pounced upon me and
very convincingly tried to pull me straight into hell. Well, I
freaked the heck out and started screaming, and pulling back.
The demons figured I was doing a great job selling it, so they
kicked their enthusiasm up a notch, and a couple more joined
in the fray. I went ballistic and thrashed around while Satan

laughed and laughed, and the demons pulled me closer to hell. After a few seconds of this, I became hysterical; the real actor ran up, and they realized they'd made a terrible mistake.

I sat practically hyperventilating in the corner as everyone tried to calm me down, and a few kids tried to stifle their laughter. I guess it would have been hilarious if it weren't you being dragged to hell, even though my screams had to have been convincing. I was really shaken up but tried to regain my brave face again. When I finally was able to move on, we walked into the next room, which was stark in contrast. It was heaven. We watched as the girl walked into a clean, beautiful, serene setting where everyone was smiling, warm, and welcoming. The music was soft, very soothing. The girl was so excited to be there, and at the end of the walkway was Jesus Himself. He walked up to her, gave her a huge hug, and welcomed her home. It was probably even more moving than hell was.

Jesus then took time to walk around and speak to each one of us, ask how we were doing, and tell us He loved us so much. It was wonderful, and I completely forgot about my recent trauma. When the play was over, we were guided into the last room, where the pastor delivered the salvation message. When he was finished, he asked if anyone wanted to accept Christ. My hand shot up instantly, and the pastor said I should confess my sins to the Lord. An usher took me into another room, where they spoke to me for a minute and congratulated me on being saved, and I was given a Bible. Then they thanked me for coming and said good-bye. That was it. *Had I really just become a Christian?* I thought to myself. *I sure hope so,* I thought as I recalled the terrifying vision of hell.

The truth is, the pastor told me to confess my sins, and I think I did. But I had no idea he also meant I was not to sin anymore. I didn't even really know what sin was! Did my attitude or behaviors change? Absolutely not. Nothing changed. I just wanted to make sure I had my spot reserved in heaven, and I did what they told me to.

Have you or someone you know had a similar experience where you went to church, raised your hand, said a prayer, and thought that was the end of it? I know this is a significant problem, especially in Western churches. We often focus on production values and get people to "pray the prayer," but then what? If you had a similar experience, did you think your relationship with God was strong and that your place in heaven was secure? Did you truly undergo a radical life change? I know for a fact I sure didn't. In fact, I didn't truly enter into a real relationship with Jesus until many years later. Yet if anyone asked me, I would have assured him or her that I was saved and had my seat reserved in heaven. I raised my hand. I prayed the prayer. I'd performed the ritual. I was good, right?

If only the tremendous responsibility and implications I'd accepted had been explained to me before I raised my hand,

I might have wasted far less time in beginning to fulfill God's purpose for my life. In Luke 14:28–33, Jesus tells us to very soberly count the cost before following Him:

> For which of you, intending to build a tower, does not sit down first and count the cost, whether he has enough to finish it—lest, after he has laid the foundation, and is not able to finish, all who see it begin to mock him, saying, "This man began to build and was not able to finish"? Or what king, going to make war against another king, does not sit down first and consider whether he is able with ten thousand to meet him who comes against him with twenty thousand? Or else, while the other is still a great way off, he sends a delegation and asks conditions of peace. So likewise, whoever of you does not forsake all that he has cannot be My disciple.

You see, what happens when we have a halfhearted experience is that we believe there is no power in the gospel. *I've experienced that. It's okay,* we tell ourselves. We don't know any better. Instead of raising our hand at an altar call and admitting we're sinners and need a Savior, we simply want to reserve our ticket into heaven. To really just avoid hell, if we're being honest. We may even settle for anywhere but hell. It may not even have to be with Jesus as long as it's relatively chill. That's the difference…it's a heart thing. Guess what happens when you don't really know what you're committing to? At the first sign of trouble, you buckle. There is no power. There is no *purpose*. We have to ask ourselves: *Do I really know God?*

The truth is, when you accept Christ, you are accepting an entire life change. When an employer hires a new employee, there are high expectations for that person; Christ is no different. He expects great things from you, because He knows what you're really capable of with His Spirit empowering you. Jesus paid a tremendous price, dying on a cross for your sins. Can you claim to be truly saved if you are still living in sin? People ask me if homosexuality is a sin, and my answer is, directly, yes. Is that sin worse than others, though? No. Adultery, lust of the eyes, greed, gossip, laziness...God counts all sin as equal. All sins grieve Him equally. *Yet how are we supposed to stop sinning and truly commit to God?* I'll show you soon.

First, I'll admit we still sin after we become Christians. Yes, it's sad but true. We were born into a sinful world, and although we strive for perfection, we will miss the mark at times. This doesn't mean that we can do whatever we want because we think God will forgive us anyway. No, that's called abusing God's grace. We are to live a life worthy of the calling He has placed on us, and that means turning from sin, but there's a secret to doing that. I promised in the last chapter that I'll show you the secret to automatically trusting God with everything, and that is related to turning from sin. In fact, you cannot stop sinning without knowing and nurturing this one, major detail.

The first step, however, as we saw in the last chapter, is always humility. In 2 Chronicles 7:14, the Lord tells us:

> If My people who are called by My name will humble themselves, and pray and seek My face, and turn from their wicked ways, then I will hear from heaven and will forgive their sin and heal their land.

Humility is always the first step. If we don't count the cost of what we're committing to, we're hanging on to a little of that stubbornness, aren't we? Our faith becomes diluted, halfhearted…lukewarm. God can't tolerate that. The spiritual world is in a life-and-death struggle for our souls, and we're halfheartedly plodding around, compromising, and waiting for "someday" because we don't know the *power* and *purpose* of what we've committed to. We don't really know God. I don't say this in the slightest to condemn you, as again, I'm in the same boat. I say this because there is a way to walk in the full purpose and power God intends for your life, and it's the most wonderful thing you've ever experienced.

Please stay with me as we wrap up this section in the next chapter. I'm going to show you how to ignite that flame in your heart and keep it burning white hot so that your life goes from glory to glory to glory and you fulfill the very purpose you were designed for, greater than you could ever dream of. And it's the most natural thing in the world. In fact, *it's what you were created for*. Let's go…

6

The Girl of My Dreams

I love it when friends tell me they are getting married. I am sure your response is similar to mine: "That's wonderful! Have you set a date? How did he propose?" It's always such an exciting time, and there seems to be nothing but joy for the happy couple. Yet I'm sure you've experienced a time or two where you're silently thinking, "Oh my goodness! Are you guys sure? Didn't you break up and get back together three times over the last six months?" It's tough to ask the genuine questions and of course, they always need to be handled with tact. But I know I would want my friends to find a way to give me a gigantic heads-up if I were to potentially make a critical choice without thinking it through. If we really wanted to be asking the genuine yet somewhat less maudlin questions, we'd be saying something like, "How do you know this is the person God has chosen for you? Did you seek Him in your decision? Do you really love this person and if so, how does your life show you do? More importantly, *does your relationship reflect your love for God*?" Hmm.

I can ask myself the same question. *Does my life show I love God? Is that even really important? Do I only love Him because it increases my chances of getting into heaven? Do I obey Him only out of fear of hell?* Of course, I'd rather go to heaven, but if I truly love God, does my life show it? And *how* does it show? For many years, I claimed to love God, but looking back, my priorities were making money, buying slick cars and big houses, and gaining popularity. None of my actions demonstrated love for God. In fact, I once had to ask a friend to be a reference for a job interview. When I went to the interview, the interviewer happened to know my friend pretty well. He had wonderful things to say about my buddy, but it soon became apparent the interviewer wasn't saying much about me. He lauded my friend as a truly godly man whose love for Jesus emanated from everything he did. Then, at the end of the interview, he looked me in the eye and gently encouraged me to be more like my friend. "You don't really show your Christianity, Dustin," he said. Ouch! I was shocked, and the statement cut me deeply. But it made me think.

Unfortunately, it wasn't the last incident of its kind. Some years later, I applied for seminary. Once again, I had to ask friends for references. One of my friends agreed to provide a reference but as the time drew closer, I realized he had never turned in the form. I asked him about it, and he just said, "It's a lot to fill out." I knew that couldn't be the only reason, so I pressed him. After a while, he admitted the questions were far more personal than he'd expected and needed to

69

be answered honestly. He told me he wasn't sure if he could answer the questions and paint me in a positive light without lying. I was stunned. *How was I living that my friend would have to lie about my faith and character?* That moment was a huge wake-up call. As we discussed it, I began to see that I had a *heart problem.* I was involved in the right groups and associated with the right people, but my life didn't serve as a testimony of my love of God. A healthy church will quickly reveal that in you, and you should appreciate it immensely! After discussing with a few people and giving it no small amount of thought and prayer, I came to see the way I acted, the way I was treating my wife, and especially my actions under pressure did not demonstrate any of the God kind of love. Thankfully, I asked myself the critical question: *Why not?*

How do you show someone you love him or her? I know in Christian circles, it's become somewhat of a cliché, but we know love is far more than an emotion. Love always begins as sacrificial, whether driven by giddy emotion or by the unbreakable bond of a parent and a child. Some of the demonstrations of love are spending time with, investing in, getting to know, and serving a person, and putting that person's needs above your own. Think about the Lord. In the last chapter, we discussed whether or not we *really* know Him. We believe He's good, and we know Jesus died for us, *but how does that go from mental assent to our living reality*?

When I speak about loving the Lord, believe me when I say (a) I'm by no means completely there yet; and (b) what I've learned, I've undoubtedly learned the hard way. I suppose the journey for me began in childhood, when my mother taught me at home in lieu of sending me to public school. At least once a month, other families who homeschooled would meet to socialize, discuss their experiences, and brainstorm. I always crossed my fingers that the other kids would be dragged to the meeting so we could hang out. I especially hoped girls would show up. While the parents discussed strategies to "effectively educate us," it was a time for the homeschooled kids to get some semblance of a social life. One night when I was thirteen years old, I was waiting outside the meeting, wearing my favorite Randy Moss football jersey, and by my own admission, looking pretty freakin' cool. I didn't have many friends, so I would often throw a football against a tree to keep myself occupied. Even as I'm writing this, many years later, I know and agree with you that I was very pathetic. If I missed the tree, I would have to run and retrieve the ball, but if I hit my mark, it would bounce back to me. In time, I got pretty good at it. This night was like many others, just waiting outside the meeting, throwing a football at palm trees.

I was just getting bored when two girls showed up. *Yes! Time to turn on the charm!* I thought. Please keep in mind that I was a chunky prepubescent kid with a bowl haircut. Total winner. Anyway, I squinted at them in the fading light and realized I knew the one girl, but as I got a closer look at the other, I realized I'd never seen her before. As she came into view, my jaw dropped open. *Holy smoke, she's hot!* The girl was absolutely gorgeous, stealing my breath away the moment I laid eyes on her. I was instantly in love. Of course, when I needed it the most, the charm evaporated, but I desperately wanted to meet this girl. For some strange reason, however, I was now too shy to walk over.

I guess I was standing there, staring at them goofily, when the supermodel called me over.

"What's your name, boy?" she asked rudely.

"Er, Dustin," I replied. *Be cool,* I chided myself. "My mom is in the meeting," my mouth said awkwardly before my brain could shut it down. I withered inside.

"Congratulations," she said sarcastically, casting a "What block of cheese did he just crawl out of?" look at her friend.

She's so witty! I thought. *It's so hot!* She asked me a few more questions, and I responded, doing my best to impress her, but after a while it became apparent she was more interested in hanging out with her friend. I tried to play it cool, so I went to sit in my mom's van and listen to music, playing it loud enough so they could hear how hip I was. Even though she didn't seem interested in me, I was certain I'd made a good impression on the girl. When the meeting was over, they went inside to help the adults clean up, while I hung back, ready to bounce my football until my mom was ready to leave. The new girl marched over to me and demanded, "What are you doing, lazy? Get over here and help us!" Startled, I jumped to attention and followed them inside like a lamb.

Oh yeah, I grinned to myself. *I could marry a girl like this.*

That girl never came back to the meetings.

Years went by, and one day I started attending a new church. One Friday night, I went to check out their youth service, and as I walked in, I saw the most beautiful girl singing on stage, and my heart skipped a beat. *Man, she looks so familiar*, I thought. I couldn't put my finger on how I knew her, but I had definitely met her before. Suddenly, we made eye contact, and it seemed as though she were trying to place me as well. When the service was over, she walked over to me; I can't recall what she said, but it was something really sarcastic. Right then and there, I remembered she was "The One," and my dormant infatuation broke free again. I was hooked, and I subsequently signed up for everything I could possibly involve myself in at that church. There was zero doubt in my mind this girl was the one I would marry, so I simply did all I knew to do. I pursued her like crazy. Whatever she wanted, I made it happen. Any whim she had, I was at her beck and call. She didn't always say thank you, and she would be sarcastic, so I would become ten times more besotted. I would have done anything for that girl. I went to every church outing, every activity, and every camp just to be near her.

As I grew into a young adult, I never gave up on my dream girl. At one point, I realized I needed to lose some weight, so I began hitting the gym for an hour or sometimes two hours every day. I was diligent. I began to cut weight and build muscle and started looking and feeling great. It was around this time, when I was spending so much time on my physical appearance, that my friends probably began realizing I was talking the talk of a Christian but was only spending maybe five minutes a day with the Lord. He wasn't nearly as much of a priority as getting into shape, and next to my dream girl, the Lord was a distant focus. That sounds pathetic when I see it on paper. I wanted to get in shape physically for my dream girl but spiritually, I was lazy and fat and out of shape. I had no idea that if I devoted my life to finding and fulfilling God's purpose for me, He would bring everything I needed that would completely fulfill me. I wasn't living an outrageously sinful life, so I stubbornly and blindly kept doing it my way.

At the age of twenty-one, I started the journey to own my own business; I was elated to become an entrepreneur! I felt blessed and full of joy, but in my heart I became a little cocky and took all of the credit. After all, I had worked hard to present myself, built the collateral, and submitted the paperwork. I thought: *Look at me! Look at what I've accomplished. I am going to prove how wonderful I am and show them they made a good choice.* At twenty-two, I opened my business and made more money than I ever thought possible. Immediately, I bought a nice car, a beautiful home, and new clothes, all of which I believed I needed. Being so young, I had zero discipline with my money and started spending like tomorrow was the end of the world.

I still told myself I was blessed by God, but as I busied myself with my new toys, business trips, and running the business, I slowly began to rely on God less and less. I felt so financially secure that I began to forget the source of my blessing. I didn't realize it, but my foundation was turning to sinking sand. Rather than remaining faithful to and pursuing God, I started chasing the dollar bill. In fact, I was chasing a million of them. I began to wonder what my life would look like if I opened a second location and how much more money I could make. I didn't think for a second if the time it would take would allow me to spend time with my Lord Jesus. My circle of friends began to change. I networked with all the important (usually nonbelieving) people in town, and they all wanted to know the young, confident entrepreneur that just opened up shop. I finally thought I was somebody. In reality, I was well on my way to becoming nobody of consequence. There are a million business owners but very few sold-out servants of God. I was rich on earth but poor in my relationship with Jesus. Predictably, I started treating people as inferior. My material possessions and social standing became among the most important things to me. Before long, my attitude and entire outlook toward life had changed.

As I think back to those times, I am reminded of a very poignant story in Luke 18:18–31, when a rich young man asked Jesus what he needed to do to get into heaven. Jesus rattled off all the commandments and told him he should keep them all. The man was waiting for this answer and confidently responded he had done so, ever since his youth. I believe the young man was there expecting Jesus to congratulate him, give him a virtual ticket to heaven, and pat him on the back for being such a successful lad. The good news was the rich young man was smart enough to realize admittance to heaven was the ultimate prize. In his mind, however, it was the last notch to etch into his belt as the supreme accomplishment, and here he believed he was about to accomplish it at the mouth of this powerful prophet who had arisen in Israel.

As the young man was probably grinning, pleased with himself for fulfilling the requirements of keeping the law, Jesus, the ultimate discerner of hearts, threw a curve ball. It cut straight to the core of the issue. Jesus told the rich young man the only remaining task was to sell everything he owned and give it to the poor. Jesus promised that in doing so, he would receive treasures in heaven. And then Jesus did something spectacular. He invited the young man to follow Him. Effectively, Jesus called the young man in the same way He had called each of His disciples. All he had to do was give up everything. Although this may seem like an unbearably difficult task for most of us, you know what? Jesus was absolutely serious. This young man could have been recorded in the Bible as one of the disciples. Who knows, perhaps he would have been the one to take Judas's place instead of Matthias (Acts 1:12–26).

Sadly, the rich young man couldn't bear to hear this news and became very disheartened. He had grown to love his wealth and "stuff" so much that it had become his identity. What would he be without all of this wealth and status? Had he worked so hard, pursued wealth so much, just to give it all away? It would quite literally be giving his identity away. That's exactly what Jesus required, because the rich young man's identity was pretty rotten. Jesus wanted to give him a fresh, fulfilling identity as His disciple. The young man, however, walked away with his head hung, unable to accept Jesus's words. Aren't we the same? If this man wanted to truly follow Jesus, he had to give up the stuff his heart was attached to. Why? Because Jesus knows we won't succeed in our calling, our purpose, if our hearts are set on anything but Him. *Why?* Because Jesus wants our motives to be pure. We generically try to define ourselves by our accumulation of status, our reputation at work, and the car we drive. Jesus will bless you with far more. He may entrust wealth to you. He may call you to the mission fields of Asia and Africa. He may do both. Whatever He does, when you trust Him with all your heart, you will be more fulfilled than you could ever have dreamed of. He will grow you and stretch you, and you will become a mighty implement of salvation in His hands. And that doesn't mean He may not give you a nice car. It just means it will only matter because the Savior you adore gave it to you as a gift, and nothing more.

Think about it. What could this young man possibly have owned that was more important than a relationship with Jesus?

The problem was he hadn't thought about it thoroughly. He hadn't prepared his heart. If Jesus commanded the same thing from any of us, would we feel the same reluctance as the rich man? If we hadn't prepared our hearts—absolutely, yes! When I bought my first house, I bought so much unnecessary furniture to fill it with. When I moved, I sold it all, so what was the point? After accumulating belongings that I didn't really need, I listed all of it for sale and moved into an apartment. I am not trying to be boastful of what I have done; I am showing you that I've accomplished the goal of riches at a young age, and it doesn't fulfill. The only thing that fulfills is obedience to Jesus Christ. There is nothing that will bring you more status, reputation, blessing, and fulfillment, yet you won't even care about that because all you'll want to do is please your Savior. God is still molding me; He is nowhere near finished with me. I still enjoy dining out and sitting on nice furniture, but every day I make it a point to keep my focus on God and not on those things. They are simply a by-product of a healthy relationship with the Lord. They're no longer the most important things in my life but rather nice perks or a neat surprise once in a while.

After receiving the loving admonishments of friends and taking a good, hard look at my life, I reached a point where I found out what it truly meant to accept Christ. To truly become a Christian, a *Christ-follower*. I began attending church for the right reasons, truly sorrowful I had wasted so many years with the wrong mind-set. I had wasted years pursuing a girl and had gained barely anything out of church. I hadn't forged a real relationship with Jesus, and my identity was fraudulent. I had been worshipping a woman instead of God. I built a relationship with this girl, and she knew I wanted to marry her more than anything else. In fact, a huge part of my motivations was likely her. Yet every time she and I got in a fight or she stopped speaking to me, I turned my back on church. I reached a point where I asked myself if was really a believer, a follower of God? In that tough moment, I came to the conclusion I didn't truly love God; I didn't even know what love for God looked like. I laid my idols down and submitted to God. When I did, everything changed.

Jesus wants your whole heart. He wants you to give up anything in your life that is preventing Him from having it. The Bible asks how a man profits if he gains the whole world but loses his soul. When you look at it that way, it really puts things into perspective. It was hard for me to balance having a good income while still trusting the Lord to provide for me. I had to be knocked off my high horse a few times before I came back to reality. *And that's okay!* God is patient; we are human. As long as we keep genuinely trying, we will make progress, and God finds that very pleasing.

I want the Lord to guide me and take care of me. I want to have a strong relationship with Jesus. He's real, and He has a real plan for my life and yours. If I have to trust in myself for everything I accomplish, I am already lost. The story about the rich young man does not end on a happy note; he was very downhearted when Jesus told him to give up his things in order to follow Him. It teaches us the gravity of the situation, however.

> And when Jesus saw that he became very sorrowful, He said, "How hard it is for those who have riches to enter the kingdom of God! For it is easier for a camel to go through the eye of a needle than for a rich man to enter the kingdom of God." (Luke 18:24–25)

Man. That is a gut-wrenching statement. *It is impossible for someone to enter heaven if they cannot give up what they have on earth to follow Jesus.* Wow! Yet, as the people began to freak out, Jesus comforted them, as He does us:

> And those who heard it said, "Who then can be saved?"

> But He said, "The things which are impossible with men are possible with God."

> Then Peter said, "See, we have left all and followed You."

> So He said to them, "Assuredly, I say to you, there is no one who has left house or parents or brothers or wife or children, for the sake of the kingdom of God, who shall not receive many times more in this present time and in the age to come eternal life." (Luke 18:26–30)

So how are we supposed to do this? God has provided a way. It's called *grace*. People have used grace as a good acronym, with which I agree: God's Riches At Christ's Expense. Jesus paid the price for us to be born of His divine nature. Once we receive Him as Lord, our spirit is reborn. We no longer desire to live in death but in life. I believe this is part of what He meant when He said, *"The things which are impossible with men are possible with God."*

"So why do I still have those desires and priorities to be rich and chase the opposite sex and live a life of ease?" you may ask. Well, that's because you aren't spending time building your relationship with Jesus.

You see, it always begins in faith, with obedience. If you're obedient to spending time with God, He has promised to heal you and save you and bless you abundantly (2 Chronicles 7:14). Prayer has almost become a taboo word these days because it brings up feelings of guilt and pressure. But prayer is not taboo; it is simply spending time with your Father, His amazing Son, and their sweet, loving Holy Spirit. Just hanging out! Does God not deserve your time and much more? How can He possibly know I love Him if I don't spend time getting to know Him? It begins by reading the Bible and praying. That's where His attributes are recorded. We also attend church faithfully, perhaps begin volunteering, and then a spectacular thing happens. *We begin to become more like Him.* It always starts in faith and obedience. You may be thinking, "Get off my back, dude," but then you're misunderstanding me. I'm trying to show you that one small step of obedience will transform your life. This is the secret I've been talking about. *Relationship.* There is nothing more powerful for a human being than to be in relationship with the all-powerful, all-loving, all-providing God. In light of that concept, consider what a joy and a privilege it is to be able to love the Lord.

When you're spending time with God every day, just speaking to Him, reading His Word, and listening for the voice of the Holy Spirit, you're building relationship. That is the foundation for what Jesus requires when He says, "Give up everything to follow Me." In light of prioritizing a daily relationship with Him, we come to know He is good and will take care of all our other needs. That's how we deal with difficult scriptures like Luke 14:25–27 (NKJV).

And there went great multitudes with him: and he turned, and said unto them,

"If any man come to me, and hate not his father, and mother, and wife, and children, and brethren, and sisters, yea, and his own life also, he cannot be my disciple.

And whosoever doth not bear his cross, and come after me, cannot be my disciple."

So what comes first in your life? As a teenager, my number one priority was pursuing a girl. Guess what? Even though I wasn't focused on Him, God still blessed me. Today, I am married to Sara, the beautiful girl of my dreams. This is a sign of God's love for me, even when I wasn't loving Him back. I have chased after other things as well—cars, toys, money, houses, and admiration. When I was starting out as a businessman, I put my business before God, yet His precious Holy Spirit kept wooing me. He pursued me while I was pursuing other things, as His extremely valued treasure. Why did He do this? Romans 2:4 says,

> Or do you despise the riches of His goodness, forbearance, and longsuffering, not knowing that the goodness of God leads you to repentance?

The goodness of God leads us to repentance. Isn't that the truth? So may I ask you: How are you filling that number one spot today? If it is filled with anything other than Jesus, I guarantee you will always remain ultimately empty. But He is pursuing you. Even as you read these words, I know He's speaking gently to your heart. When we put God first in our lives, everything else will fall into place. He created you, and He knows what will fulfill you. Primarily that is a relationship with Him, and all good things are born out of that.

I can talk about it all day long, but without you taking that step of action and making the time to sit down and spend time with your Savior, you'll never really know what I'm talking about. He knows our hearts' true desires. He sees what we long for, and He wants us to have good things. He also has the ultimate blueprint for your life that will blow away your wildest dreams. We know we are making progress when we pursue Him in our actions, our thoughts, and our words. I am so happy that God knows what He is doing and I don't have to be in charge of everything. It's stressful trying to be responsible for every detail in your life. It's also futile.

Ask yourself right now: What is holding you back from following Christ with your full heart? Make a list and then review it. Next, come up with a plan for how you can re-structure your priorities to make Jesus number one. There is truly nothing more important in this earthly life than your relationship with God. I assure you, our treasures are not on earth. Of course, there are fun and exciting things to partake of here, but they are nothing compared to knowing the Creator and all that He has in store for you. Can you do that? Can you be honest with yourself about your priorities and then have the courage to change? God has planned an abundant, fulfilling life for you. He has a future full of hope and opportunities waiting. Whatever you are putting in front of Him is hindering you, so don't hold back anything from Him today.

That's the big secret my friend. *Relationship.* There is noth-ing more important and nothing more powerful. When you know your God, that's when the power kicks in, and His is a *lasting love.* I know this doesn't happen overnight. It takes small steps. Steps of action. That's why I've written the next section for you. Let's check it out...

Section 2

Take Action

We've laid the foundation of examining our motives and know that at the very least, God has something much more for us. Now, the following section is written to take you to the depths of your motives and examine them thoroughly. Once you surface, I believe you will realize there are changes that need to be made—changes that may be difficult at first, but with your faith based on a *relationship* with the one, true God, the journey to fulfillment will become far easier as you progress.

This middle section is where a lot of the "heavy lifting" change will be done. I will expand on the concepts of refocusing your life into what matters to God and how to do it. As you've now been woken from your slumber and begun to refocus your life by developing a far deeper relationship with God, He will begin to allow you to be tested further. There are very real struggles in life, and this section will show you how to approach those struggles. Although life is often a challenge, you will see that not only can we take joy in trials as the proving of our faith produces patience, but after every trial comes a promotion and a reward.

This section's purpose is to encourage you to take steps to actively participate in a deep relationship with God.

Let us begin.

7

Sex, Drugs, and Mexican Cartels

My father-in-law, Bill, is one of the godliest men I know. Bill has probably forgotten about more work he's done for the kingdom of God than most of us could hope to accomplish. Fighting human trafficking, serving the homeless, and helping addicts of all kinds, Bill has also pioneered several ministries and changed countless lives. He also founded several churches in the United States and Guatemala. Bill walks an authentically righteous walk.

When you first meet him, all you'll see is a pretty typical older, white, middle-class gentleman with salt-and-pepper hair. The lines and creases seen in his face could well be from a life spent in traditional mission fields, doing traditional ministry work. Yet never for a moment would you imagine Bill's testimony. You'd never guess what Bill's "rock bottom" was, when he chose to cry out to God for rescue. You'd never dream how God began to use this once majorly lost sheep to rescue others in turn.

Bill was born in Denver, Colorado, and his parents, along with much of his extended family, owned local bars in the area. This was his family's legacy and their profession. They were good at it, knew their hustle, and were people the locals knew not to cross. Naturally, as a child, Bill spent a lot of time in bars, and just some of what he was exposed to included gambling, pornography, spousal abuse, and of course, severe alcoholism. Bill knew nothing else, but like we all do, he felt a yearning as a young man to fill a deep, unidentifiable void in his life.

At the tender age of sixteen, he moved out of his parents' home, taking his chances in the world. Bill was not prepared nor was he equipped to deal with the responsibility of adulthood. Unsurprisingly, he jumped from job to job, often lasting only a day or two because of his poor work ethic and sour attitude. Eventually, Bill clawed his way to a semblance of a sustainable life and even managed to begin classes at the University of Colorado. When the struggles and pressures of work, school, and real life hit him like a tsunami, Bill turned to what he knew best: alcoholism. He began perpetuating the paradigm he so desperately wanted to escape, and in maddening frustration, started lashing out at the world. He was subsequently arrested on five different occasions. Bill would also never graduate from the university.

Beginning to feel hopeless and struggling to find work, he decided to try a completely different life and booked a ticket to Nogales, Mexico. Although he was an unmistakable *gringo*,

Bill had a way with Mexican locals, and soon he discovered an opportunity at a Samsonite luggage plant. Bill didn't realize that in Mexico, "opportunities" were rarely lucky or the result of one's irresistible charm. The foreman said he had just the job for Bill and placed him on the line, where he was to fasten pieces of luggage together with giant staples. At the last minute, his supervisor told Bill that most people only lasted a week in the position. When Bill asked why, the guy chuckled, gestured, and said, "They always staple their hand to the luggage. So be careful, hey?" What the foreman didn't realize was how desperate Bill was, so he shook his head and smiled at the crazy *gringo*, as Bill accepted with a happy grin.

Bill was determined to make it work. He was careful in his work and made sure he lasted a week. Then he lasted two. Then he lasted a month, and then a year. During that time, Bill became a fixture in the community, and his tenacity, intellect, and willingness to succeed caught the eye of the Samsonite brass. Bill began moving on up in the world and soon had money to spare. Life was looking good. He began socializing more, getting to know the big players in Nogales. Before long, Bill was partying with one of the leaders of the largest Mexican drug cartel at the time. The man took a huge shining to Bill, and they became firm friends. Bill's life would subsequently take a tremendous moral dive.

He continued to be diligent with his work, though, knowing the value of escaping one's predetermined plight. He ascended higher and higher in the Samsonite ranks over the next few years. Bill worked hard, and he definitely played hard, but it was in his playing with the cartel that he began to have some heavy-duty experiences. Bill was slowly introduced to what on the surface looked like a dream come true for his carnal appetites. Soon enough, however, he began to get glimpses of what was a glamorously painted viper's pit of drugs, prostitution, and *murder*. Bill knew it was time to make some choices. Before him lay the choice to turn away from this life of complicit abuse, facing a life of potentially boring loneliness, and the choice to turn a blind eye and partake. Bill chose to turn a blind eye.

Despite the excesses of his personal life, Bill's career continued to flourish. He was rapidly becoming a successful businessman, albeit by the grace of God, which he had zero concept of at the time. Bill was now traveling around the world, doing business in China, Singapore, and Russia. In his invigorated professional excellence, Bill began learning the languages of the nations he did business with. Before long, he was an authentic polyglot, speaking seven languages. It was a duality of lives, of course, as Bill's alter ego was seeing increasingly hair-raising stuff, not the least of which were having a rifle shoved into his stomach (more than once) and witnessing more and more illegal activities. This was the life he'd chosen, and Bill was sinking deeper into the quicksand one party at a time.

Bill continued ascending the Samsonite corporate ladder until he ultimately oversaw the plant where he'd been originally hired at to staple luggage together. He'd sure lasted more than a week, but he was far removed from the relatively innocent kid eager to do anything to survive. The cracks began to show. Bill's conscience had been seared over time after continually witnessing and being surrounded by international prostitution, rampant sexual deviance, and violent crime that became part of his daily life. Things reached a boiling point, and Bill began to sense it was a matter of time before his choices would cost him his life. He'd been holding it together, but fourteen years was a long time to evade consequence, and he knew he couldn't stay at Samsonite and avoid the cartel. It was time, once again, to escape.

Bill began searching for new work, and due to his now-proficient business acumen, Bill landed a position working for a billionaire. At first, this seemed like a welcome relief, as he continued to travel the globe, make ridiculous amounts of money, and meet powerful people. But as they tend to do unless you make that decision to change, Bill's problems followed him. Soon, despite his improved position, Bill found himself surrounded again by drugs, sex, and alcoholism. Bill's deepest fear was now gnawing continually at his soul. *What if there is no escape?*

The emptiness and loneliness of sin continued to drain him and one night, Bill's terrors overtook him. Hopelessness descended over him like a plastic shroud, suffocating any glimmer of optimism from his heart. With despair's tentacles wrapped firmly around his soul, Bill made the decision to take his own life. He chugged a bottle of bourbon and resigned to die. God had other plans for Bill, however, and he somehow survived. Realizing the significance of his second chance, the next day, Bill vowed to quit drinking and using drugs and to live a better life. It was truly an act of God, rather than the power of man, but Bill's choice was the catalyst. Being oblivious of spiritual things, however, Bill was now a spiritually marked man and still had a long way to go. But God is faithful; He always keeps trying and trying.

Bill's mother had since turned to Christ, and after a conversation with him, she sent him a Bible. At first, he started reading four pages each night. From an outsider's perspective, he appeared to be doing well. He still had material possessions, three homes, two cars, and a good job. This was a life many of us would be envious of, but the more Bill read, the more he realized why this life was completely unsatisfying.

At this point, I want to highlight something: *Bill took a small action step.* He knew God had spared his life, and even if in a small way, Bill took action. He took a step toward God and read those four pages a night. God responded, and Bill took another step. The steps were tiny at first, but they doubled in momentum. Bill kept taking the right steps, and the momentum toward his purpose kept building. Over the next six years, Bill would read his Bible five times, cover to cover. As a result of what he was reading, he started attending a church in Texas. At the age of thirty-five, Bill's action steps toward God culminated in the most significant decision of his life: he met Jesus Christ and gave his life completely to Him. If ever the scripture Jeremiah 29:11 was applicable, Bill's case was it:

> "For I know the plans I have for you," declares the Lord, "plans to prosper you and not to harm you, plans to give you hope and a future."

At church, Bill met his lovely future wife, Lynn, and started attending Dallas Baptist University. Soon, his new wife fell pregnant with their first child (a beautiful baby girl named Sara!). Bill heard about a mission trip to Brazil and quickly signed up. He ended up going back twice. You see, Bill acknowledged he had been unwittingly serving Satan for so many years, and as he had been diligent in his work to secular corporations, he became even more diligent to serving the kingdom of God. Unlike many of us, Bill knew he was completely hopeless without God. When he found Jesus Christ, he knew he had the answer. He knew what despair and hellish separation from God looked like. From there, it was a no-brainer to keep making the right decisions. *Why would you do otherwise?*

In time, God called their family to move around to several places before they landed in San Diego. There, Bill helped found Pathways Community Church, a ministry where Bill began to work with the lost, the hopeless, and the downtrodden. After three years in San Diego, he transferred to Saint

Petersburg, Florida, where he started a church by the same name in Largo, Florida.

Since the inception of the church, Bill has helped establish five other churches in Florida, North Carolina, Tennessee, and Guatemala. He has worked with the three largest homeless organizations in Pinellas County, Florida, and is connected with some of the largest human trafficking prevention organizations in America. Where Bill had once been complicit in the trafficking of women and drugs, God now used him to free those in bondage from those evils. Additionally, the church started a prison ministry, where they lead Bible studies with incarcerated men and women, and the church was instrumental in implementing a Celebrate Recovery program to free those trapped in the cycle of substance addiction. Bill has helped other churches in the nation implement the program as well, compounding the effect of the ministry.

I know not everyone is equipped with such a servant's heart to reach the people the world deems hopeless, but the message is that Bill was and is *willing*. That willingness leads to unquestioning action. Bill has absolutely no problem getting out of bed to pick up an intoxicated person who needs a safe place to sleep and sober up and to connect them with a solid support network. He sees the good in people when they can't even see the good in themselves. He knows that even a drunk man has a story, and that Jesus can use him in mighty ways when he is healthy and transformed by the Lord's power. Bill doesn't overlook people because of their current circumstances. He knows their hearts and wants to chase after them because that is exactly what Jesus would do. *He knows it is exactly what Jesus did for him.*

For years, I've watched this man live a life I envy (in the best way possible). When Bill graduates to heaven, God will undoubtedly look at him and say, "Well done, good and faithful servant" (Matthew 25:21). Hearing those words is a true desire of my heart. I want to life a live worthy of the calling that God has given me. I want to arrive in heaven and hear my Savior tell me I did a good job. I'd never want to hear Him say, "Dustin, you could've done more." I don't want to leave any stone unturned. I want to reach the unreachable.

What do you want God to say to you when you inevitably die and go to heaven? I know you want Him to be proud of you, embrace you, and thank you for the work you have done for the kingdom. Can I ask you today if you're taking the steps necessary to make that happen? Are you serving Jesus with your whole heart? Bill had to overcome many hurts and give up many bad habits to fully serve the Lord. He had to trust God's leading, which meant moving several times and giving up a stable career to be a full-time pastor. Are you ready to give up all that you have so God can use you? I think we hear about dramatic testimonies and instant conversions and forget about the small choices that got those people there. It's the little steps we take in the right direction that, if we keep taking them, culminate in miraculous change. What small action step can you take today to build momentum for tomorrow?

8

A Leap of Faith

I hate tests. I am probably one of the worst test takers in history. As soon as you place a test in front of me, my mind immediately begins to wander, and I find it difficult to concentrate. I typically try to focus on one question at a time, but then I get sucked into thinking about the rest of the test or reading ahead and bouncing around the questions. That carries through to most written tasks for me, and even now, rather than focusing all of my energy on writing this book, I am thinking about other things I have to do. For those reasons and so many others, I hate tests.

Tests, of course, are crucial. They ensure you understand what you have been taught, and tests prepare you for the next step. If I had never taken a test in school, how would I know if I passed a grade or absorbed any knowledge? It proves we have achieved a certain level of accomplishment and can be appropriately moved to the next level. I think while so many of us admire men like my father-in-law, Bill, in all honesty, the only thing that really sets us apart from people like that is our willingness to endure and overcome tests.

I'm sure you've heard that God will sometimes test us. It's true, but the tests God allows us to go through are for a spiritual purpose and always test our heart (spirit). God is probably not going to ask me to run the four-hundred-meter dash, but He will put tests in my path to see where my heart is at. We see a great example of this in Matthew 14:22–33, when Jesus asks Peter to join Him in walking on water:

> Immediately Jesus made His disciples get into the boat and go before Him to the other side, while He sent the multitudes away. And when He had sent the multitudes away, He went up on the mountain by Himself to pray. Now when evening came, He was alone there. But the boat was now in the middle of the sea, tossed by the waves, for the wind was contrary.

> Now in the fourth watch of the night, Jesus went to them, walking on the sea. And when the disciples saw Him walking on the sea, they were troubled, saying, "It is a ghost!" And they cried out for fear. But immediately Jesus spoke to them, saying, "Be of good cheer! It is I; do not be afraid." And Peter answered Him and said, "Lord, if it is You, command me to come to You on the water." So He said, "Come." And when Peter had come down out of the boat, he walked on the water to

go to Jesus. But when he saw that the wind was bois-terous, he was afraid; and beginning to sink, he cried out, saying, "Lord, save me!" And immediately Jesus stretched out His hand, and caught him, and said to him, "O you of little faith, why did you doubt?" And when they got into the boat, the wind ceased. Then those who were in the boat came and worshiped Him, saying, "Truly You are the Son of God."

Jesus could've calmed the storm or guided the boat back to-ward the shore, but He didn't. Instead, He took the opportu-nity to test Peter's faith. The disciples were terrified when they saw Jesus walking on water, but I have to ask why. They had witnessed His miracles before. They had seen Him heal the blind and crippled and even raise the dead. I think they still didn't *expect* to see miracles, however. Jesus, of course, had patience with them. Although He had proven Himself time and again, Jesus's disciples still struggled with their faith. But that didn't stop Him from testing them.

Determined to prove the depth of his faith when Jesus beckoned, Peter stepped out onto the water. At first, he was confident in the Lord, but when he looked at the choppy waves, focusing on them instead of Jesus, Peter's faith began to falter. It's interesting to note here that he *began* to sink. He didn't suddenly drop like a stone into the ocean; he slow-ly began sinking. How often have we taken our eyes off the Lord and subsequently lost our faith during a battle or a tough situation? When we start to sink, we suddenly remember Jesus and, falling to our knees, cry, "Lord, save me! Help me! Rescue me!" I'd guess it happens more than we'd like to admit.

When Peter began to sink, Jesus reached out His hand and saved him. Jesus was right there, but Peter had sadly failed or at least partially failed the test. How difficult it must have been for Peter to feel Jesus's, even slight disappointment. And what a bitter pill to swallow for those of us with such little faith that we begin to sink, even with Jesus's Holy Spirit living right inside us. The things that cause our faith to waver are so tiny to God. When something goes awry or gets difficult, we lose our footing, begin sinking, and desperately cry out for God to save us. Of course, He does because He is God and loves us so deeply, but as a parent, I know He smiles and asks, "O you of little faith, why did you doubt?" A friend of mine just used this story in a message at church a couple of weeks ago, and he made a great point that I had never considered. He said the tragedy was not that Peter started sinking; rather, it was that the eleven other disciples never climbed out of the boat.

Something else important to notice here is Jesus never left Peter's side. Peter was never truly in danger. Unfortunately for him, however, he was so focused on his fear that Peter was unable to see Jesus had it all under control. In fact, I think that's what the real test was. Jesus was right there, and Peter still wobbled in his faith. I relate to this passage on such a deep level, though. How often do I lose my faith when times are hard? I know mentally that Jesus is right there, but I fall, cry out on my knees, and then God picks me up and dusts me off, and I praise Him. It's a vicious cycle I have to break. Am I the only one who struggles with this? Do you do this too? It is inevitable we will fall, but you know, despite Jesus's gentle but firm assessment of Peter's faith, I believe He was still proud of him. I'll explain why.

As a teenager, I signed up to run an obstacle course with a group of adults. I was confident in my athleticism and knew I would be able to finish, and of course I proceeded to tell everyone so. In fact, I was so self-assured that I offered to train the other competitors before I'd even seen the course. The final obstacle made me wish I'd kept my mouth shut. In front of us loomed a gigantic telephone pole we were instructed to climb. Once we reached the top, we had to balance on a small platform and then jump off and try to grab a trapeze bar, while someone controlling a safety harness managed our descent if we missed.

I gazed up at this pole, and my stomach dropped. Climbing the pole and balancing on top would be challenging enough, but we were also required to turn 180 degrees once we reached the top. Now, I wear size-eleven shoes, and that pole was so narrow that I knew there was no way the platform would be wide enough for both of my water-skis to fit, let alone turn around. If you're still not sure why I may have seemed like a scared child (because after all, what's so scary about climbing up a pole?), it gets worse. The girl holding the safety harness only weighed about 110 pounds and, to top it off, I was a bit overweight. Accordingly, I was terrified to attempt this challenge and was convinced this obstacle would be the death of me.

As we completed each obstacle in the course, the dread mounted. Slowly but surely, I had to face the fact that I would soon have to deal with that last obstacle. We ran up to the telephone pole as a group, and an internal panic sprang up within me. I thought quickly and encouraged my teammates to take their turns before me, in the hope we'd run out of time so I wouldn't have to participate. Everyone seemed just as scared as I was, so I somehow maintained my game face and continued to encourage them to push past their fears and do this last obstacle. The first guy clambered up the crossbars, gingerly balanced on the platform, turned his 180, and then launched off the top of it to the cheers and applause of our teammates. This made me even more terrified. The guy was a lot smaller and more nimble than I was. There was no way I was going to make that climb. I sweated more bullets as each minute and teammate passed, my turn slowly creeping up on me. First, one person noticed my anxiety, and then another, and soon others started to realize what was up.

Eventually, even the last little girl had completed the obstacle. *So much for running out of time.* I grimaced. Mr.

Teenage Obstacle Course Trainer was faced with a decision: break down in tears, admitting I was too afraid to complete the obstacle, or take the first step and see how it went. The second option seemed like madness, but having a mental breakdown in front of everyone seemed like a slightly more dire option. I gazed up the pole, gritted my teeth, and then grabbed the crossbars. I took the first step. My team roared. Then I took another. Somehow, the shouts and cheers of my team helped me take a third. Then a fourth and pretty soon, I was almost at the top. Then I made the mistake of looking down. My team looked like ants, and I nearly threw up. I clutched the pole and closed my eyes. *Please, Lord Jesus, help me!* Going all that way back down was not even an option, so I decided to keep going.

Somehow, I made it to the top and soon realized that although there were crossbars for my feet and hands, this tall, skinny pole with this slightly chubby kid perched atop it would naturally sway in the wind. As I clung to the swaying pole, it slowly dawned on me that I *had* to climb to the top. I couldn't bail from that side of the pole, and I would have to get up and climb onto that platform. Quivering, I inched up onto the platform and finally dragged myself up. Kneeling, I swallowed hard, looked down, and immediately thought, *I shouldn't have done that.* I looked at the girl in charge of the safety harness and realized I was nearly double her weight. There was no way she'd be able to keep me from falling and, in fact, I'd probably end up killing us both. (Note to self: go on diet.)

In that moment, as I knelt there, frozen, clutching that platform, my teammates' shouts echoing around me, I realized I would have to take a leap of faith. Everyone else who had gone before me had survived, so the odds seemed to be that it was possible I might not die. I suddenly realized I couldn't allow myself to overthink it, because then I would never jump. I really had no choice but to trust this girl's ability to keep me alive and have a little faith, taking the leap.

So I did. I jumped, and I missed that trapeze bar. But the girl caught me, and guess what? I survived. (I also passed the test of completing that obstacle course!)

I believe this is why Jesus was proud of Peter. Peter's style was so "leap before you look" that he had already jumped out of the boat before considering what it was going to be like in the middle of those giant waves. True, that method has its downsides, but Peter didn't overthink it; he just trusted Jesus. Sure, he definitely freaked out when he was out in the middle of those waves, but Jesus caught him. How many times do we need to have a little more faith when it's our turn to jump off the telephone pole or jump out of the boat into the raging sea? Mentally, I knew the worst that could have happened was that I would jump off that pole and break my ankles, or maybe get the wind knocked out of me, but fear has torment, though. Although I knew I needed to jump, I also needed to know someone was there to catch me when I did.

We often fail to remember God when something frightening is thrust upon us. Peter could do anything while he was focused on Jesus. We even see this play out during Jesus's arrest in the garden of Gethsemane. But as soon as some unexpected things happened and Peter found himself in the high priest's courtyard, with three people insisting he was a friend of the man on trial, he cursed, denying he knew Jesus. Peter had taken his focus off his King again. Even so, Jesus would still rescue Peter and restore him to ministry. Jesus will always be there to catch us when we fall. He's there in the scary, dark, and lonely times. What's more, He's there in the happy, joyful, and wonderful times, too. He is *always* there. So as we walk with Him, let us walk boldly and with confidence, knowing that we aren't alone.

You may ask, "Yeah, but how do we really do that, Dustin?" Consider this scenario: I believe many of us feel as though we are stuck on a desert island, alone. Think of Tom Hanks in *Castaway*. He found himself washed up on an island in the South Pacific, and all he had was Wilson, his trusty volleyball. What if, in your hypothetical scenario, you have a Bible instead of a volleyball? You read it every day, over and over, because it is all you have to pass the time. You don't have any other books to compare it to, any commentaries to read, or any other religious writings. After a significant amount of time has passed, you are found and rescued. How strong would your faith would be? Jesus called Peter to step out of his boat in the middle of a storm and walk across the water to Him. Would you have such a strong faith after studying the Bible so deliberately and with no distractions? I am certain you would. Why? Because focusing on Jesus would become second nature to you. When you read the Bible regularly and pray, your faith is strengthened. Your knowledge of your Creator will increase, and you build your relationship with God. That is how you build your faith. That is how you build you focus on Christ. Yet again, it comes down to relationship. Relationship builds trust.

When this gets deep down inside of you, you never have to act or react in fear. You know absolutely that God has your life in the palm of His hand. He says that if you have faith even the size of a mustard seed, you can move mountains. He can accomplish more than you can dream with just a little faith. That's why, despite his shortcomings, Peter went on to lead the early church. Have you heard the saying, "God doesn't call the equipped, He equips the called?" This saying brings me comfort, and it should to you too. I don't have to have it all together or have all the answers in order for God to use me or direct my life. I just have to take the leap of faith.

If it is still a struggle to fully grasp this, consider a marriage. I think a lot about my wife, and I (usually) know what makes her happy. Like most women, she loves purses and jewelry, but after our years of marriage, I am certain those material things aren't as important to her as spending time with me. (Now, she might have a different answer, but stay with me.) Do I need to provide for her? Absolutely. Would she like an endless supply of dark chocolate? Obviously. What about a nice car or a lavish home? Sure, those things are great, but I know she would give them up if it meant losing time with me. We joined hands in marriage to walk as partners and spend our lives (time) together, not to acquire material wealth. Our relationship with God is no different. All He really wants from us is our time. Yes, you may give oodles of money to charity or volunteer at church on Sundays, but none of that matters to God as much as your relationship with Him. Because that's where you grow—in the presence of your King.

So we see that God sometimes allows circumstances to test our faith. Ask yourself right now if you are prepared. Are you ready to walk on water, through a storm in the middle of the night, if that is what He asks you to do? You'll know whether or not you believe when you're certain of your answer. Are you ready for your next test? It's inevitable, but you can be sure Jesus will be right there with you. Are you prepared for what He may call you to do? I pray you are ready to take that leap of faith and move on to the next level of your purpose.

So what happens when we start passing tests, though? When we start feeling like we've got the hang of this whole Christian walk? Oh, trust me—that's when the *real* tests only begin to take place. I hate to admit it, but I have unfortunately received that diploma from the School of Hard Knocks too...

9

Your Epitaph

I've mentioned this before, but once I became a business-man, I saw some large returns on investments and was blessed to come into some money. Let me state, however, that prior to opening my business, my wife, brother, and I were living in an apartment, refusing to turn on the air conditioning in the height of summer in order to save money. We also literally lived off ramen and McDonald's and had practically nothing in our bank account, and as the provider, I felt tremendous stress. God has always taken care of us, in a variety of ways, but that was a very scary time for my family and I. Maybe that fear, coupled with being young and naive and not knowing a thing about proper financial management, led me to spend like crazy when I finally did start making a decent paycheck. You know how they say, "Too much of a good thing is a bad thing," or "The love of money is the root of all evil?" A surplus of resources will always bring with it significant challenges. These challenges almost always revolve around matters of the heart. When I say "of the heart," I am speaking specifically of motives and motivations.

> Rejoice, O young man, in your youth,
> And let your heart cheer you in the days of your youth;
> Walk in the ways of your heart,
> And in the sight of your eyes;
> But know that for all these
> God will bring you into judgment.
> (Ecclesiastes 11:9)

As a young man, my primary motivations were to make a ton of money and to marry Sara. In the scripture above, Solomon, in his unique and Godly wisdom, states in a sagely way that it is good to pursue our hearts' desires. He ends the verse, however, with a fairly jolting admonition that, for everything we do, God will hold us accountable. Basically, he's saying, "Youth (passion plus ignorance) is no excuse." Solomon is warning us there are potential pitfalls to pursuing our hearts' desires. I wish I had understood more about this scripture as a young man.

When I started making "real money" from my first restaurant, I soon began to believe it was my own intellect, ambition, and hard work that had afforded me such success. Of course, without hard work and discipline, I would never have been able to accomplish what I did, but I forgot that God required more of me. I was young, so I suppose many people would have said my attitude was forgivable, but I imagine those same people would whisper I was precocious and might have even been secretly awaiting my downfall. In fact, some people were not so secretive about it and bluntly told me that to my face!

After I had settled into my new lifestyle, I began to showboat, taking ultimate credit for what the Lord had given me. The first thing I did after several months of a steady, healthy income was buy a Mercedes-Benz. I'll never forget the feeling that car afforded me as a young guy, rolling up to a meeting or a nice restaurant in my luxury ride. People just looked at me differently and treated me differently. I could feel status dripping off of me as I'd toss the keys to a valet attendant, believing the car earned me respect and admiration. (It did in a superficial sense to superficial people.) Boy, I absolutely *loved* to show that car off, and I came to adore the attention it drew. Pretty soon, I figured, *Why not double my charm?* I decided I needed another Mercedes. Soon after that, I bought a decadent home. It was so much more than what we needed at the time, but I felt proud when our friends gushed at how beautiful the views were and joked about moving in. Pretty soon, I had completely forgotten to give any credit or show any appreciation to God. I was living for myself and, predictably, cracks began to show. Despite my considerable income, I was living right on the edge of my means. Amazingly, I told myself I couldn't afford to give to God.

> And you shall remember the Lord your God, for it is He who gives you power to get wealth, that He may establish His covenant which He swore to your fathers, as it is this day. (Deuteronomy 8:18)

In contrast, Truett Cathy, the late founder of Chick-fil-A, was one of the most extraordinary people I have ever met. Sadly, he passed away in 2014, the year this book was started, but he will always stand out as one of my lifetime heroes. Truett had the humblest of beginnings and endured a world war but against all odds, he built a multibillion-dollar empire among scores of other competitive quick-service restaurant chains. From the start, Truett was always highly vocal about his faith, and the billionaire taught Sunday school in his home church for over fifty years. Truett professed the Bible was his guidebook and claimed to have built his business by trusting God's leading every step of the way, embodying the scripture above. Truett had a long and extremely blessed life but was probably the most humble person I have ever met. Truett never showboated. He was one of the most generous people I have encountered.

In 1946, Truett started his first company, called the Dwarf House. Having just returned home from World War II, Truett set to work building the business with his brother, Ben. They named the new restaurant the Dwarf House. Creative indeed. Truett devised the revolutionary idea to debone a chicken breast, pressure-cook it, and serve it on a sandwich. Although the restaurant was small, it was a hit from the start.

In 1967, Chick-fil-A was born. (By the way, If you have never had a Chick-fil-A sandwich, put down this book immediately, drive to your nearest location, order a chicken sandwich, waffle fries, lemonade, and Chick-fil-A sauce, and discover this magical world of flavor and pure joy.) Aside from the aforementioned deliciousness, there are several things I love about this company. First, Chick-fil-A took a chance on a young entrepreneur and gave me an astounding opportunity, for which I will always be grateful. Second, I love that Chick-fil-A is a $6 billion (and growing!) company that is completely debt free. They have achieved this feat by adhering to the principle Truett held since the beginning: honor God with all you do. The leadership of the company strives to be excellent stewards of everything God has entrusted to them, and they pass that down to the franchisees. What an amazing business mentality, especially in these times of cutthroat corporate tactics. It makes me truly proud to be a part of this fascinating company. I believe the secret is clinging to Truett's original, godly motives.

Lastly, one of the reasons I respect Truett Cathy so much is that every single one of over *seventeen hundred* locations is closed on Sundays. Although Sunday is statistically one of the most profitable days for restaurants, Truett displayed obedience to God by providing this sacred day of rest and family time for himself and his team. Team members love this policy because they are always guaranteed a day off. I believe this in turn generally attracts a more sensible team. This true pioneer's forethought and mind-set still blow me away. His motivations were to honor God, love people, and work hard. From the very beginning, Truett understood that money is unquestionably not everything.

As a result, despite every Chick-fil-A location being closed every Sunday, they became the "largest quick-service chicken restaurant chain in the United States[1]." That distinction tells me God blessed this man and continues to bless Chick-fil-A because of his faithfulness. The blessing overflows to all aspects of the company. And Truett's love for God didn't end with his company; he also maintained a special place in his heart for children. Chick-fil-A's Lifeshape Foundation owns and operates many foster homes around the nation, and for many of these orphans, these houses will be their "forever home" until they reach adulthood.

At the yearly Chick-fil-A seminars, when Truett walked out on the stage, I was always moved to tears by the response of the crowd. Everyone went wild. They would stand, applaud, and cheer for what seemed like an eternity, all because they wanted to show gratitude toward this man. Did they hold him in such high esteem simply because he created a chicken sandwich? No. He earned that reaction because of how he glorified God with that chicken sandwich and subsequently created opportunities for a better life in all areas. Truett's faith was so strong it was *visible*. He did not always have a thriving business, and he had definitely battled his share of difficulties. In his books, you can read about each time the business could have failed, but Truett chose to honor God no matter what and trust God knew what He was doing. (I strongly encourage you to read one of the multiple books this inspirational man has written, to get a more complete picture of his amazing legacy.)

I pray I reach the point in my life where I honor God in all circumstances as Truett Cathy did, and I pray you can too. In reality, however, I am still a major work in progress, and the most blatant example of showboating I am personally guilty of sadly (and ironically) occurred at the 2010 Chick-fil-A annual seminar. As was tradition, Truett came out on stage, and everyone applauded for some time. Truett silenced the crowd in modesty, and as the hush fell over the audience, he announced he was going to do something out of the ordinary. He said he wanted to auction something off to benefit the LifeShape charity, and he called up his friend, a famous auctioneer. He then removed his wristwatch for the man to sell.

Truett, of course, is a legend, and many people jumped at the chance to own something that belonged to him. The auctioneer started the bidding at $100. It quickly shot to a bid of $1,000, and then in the blink of an eye, it hit the $2,000 mark. I glanced at my wife, and she looked at me quizzically. Then I did something crazy. I raised my hand and jumped headlong into the auction. Only as I saw myself on the huge overhead screen did I realize I was one of two nut jobs who had agreed to pay *$3,000* for this simple wrist watch. I suddenly had a dreadful sense that after the event, Sara would call an attorney to draw up divorce papers. Still, something kept me bidding.

I wanted that watch because it was Truett's, but if I'm honest with myself, I also wanted to show people that although I was the new kid in town, I could easily afford it. There were more than three thousand people in that room, watching me bid on that watch, but as I look back on that day, I realize what an idiot I had been. The bidding soared: $3,200, $3,500, $3,750…eventually, I bid $4,000, and my stomach flipped a little as the final call went once…went twice…and then ended with the auctioneer shouting a loud, "SOLD!" I glanced nervously at my wife, whose jaw was on the floor in shock. She couldn't murder me right there in front of the thousands of eyes locked on us, but I knew it could well have happened if we were alone. I won that watch for the low, low tag of $4,000. Truett called me up on stage, and I shook his hand as I accepted the watch. I grinned to hide a grimace as he explained he had purchased the watch at Walgreens in 1980 for $9.75. I was suddenly sick to my stomach. I had spent four grand on something that was over thirty years old and worth less than $10. Sure, I relished the sentiment of the item, but the joy was soured by my conscience squawking that I had really spent $4,000 to impress a crowd of strangers.

To add insult to injury, I couldn't even tell you where that watch is now. It's somewhere in my house, in a closet or a box, but it isn't displayed in all of its $4,000 splendor. I look back on that day knowing I didn't honor God with that purchase because my motives were purely self-serving. Yeah, it was a once-in-a-lifetime experience, and I am now known at the annual seminar as the Watch Guy, but I should have used that money in a far more pragmatic way. I'm not saying it's always wrong to do things like that. I'm sure the money was used for some wonderful cause, but my point is that I did it for the wrong reasons. My heart was impure, and that's what causes regret. When others examine my life, I want them to say that I have honored God with everything that has been given to me from this point on. Wouldn't that be an outstanding epitaph? "He glorified God with everything he had." Don't you want that too?

What would it take to achieve this feat, though? Of having an epitaph—a life statement—that glorifies God? When we're considering our motivations, I believe it's very helpful to have some sort of measuring stick. What is "enough" when considering what we need to give to God? The answer might surprise you.

Now Jesus sat opposite the treasury and saw how the people put money into the treasury. And many who were rich put in much. Then one poor widow came and threw in two mites, which make a quadrans.

So He called His disciples to Himself and said to them, "Assuredly, I say to you that this poor widow has put in more than all those who have given to the treasury; for they all put in out of their abundance, but she out of her poverty put in all that she had, her whole livelihood." (Mark 12:41–44)

This old, poor widow gave everything she had. Literally. She probably resigned to starve, figuring two mites (about two dollars' worth of currency) wasn't going to keep her alive very long, so she likely reasoned it was better to give it to God. Her motives were completely in the right place, and I don't believe for a second that Jesus allowed her to starve. In this profound example, Jesus says the rich, who put in much money (and did so very publicly, it seems) barely gave anything compared to this widow. Jesus is making a major statement in this passage. He is saying as clear as day that it is not what we necessarily give but *what we keep* that determines our motives.

I am embarrassed to admit I used to tell people how much I gave to this charity or that organization. This is not what God wants. Matthew 6:3 says, "But when you give to the needy, do not let your left hand know what your right hand is doing."

Two verses prior, in Matthew 6:1, Jesus said, "Be careful not to practice your righteousness in front of others to be seen by them."

I would love going to charity auction events not for the opportunity to support a worthy cause but because whatever I spent was a tax write-off. I also went because people looked at the big spenders with reverence and respect, and I craved that feeling. I wanted to earn my place in these social circles and prove I deserved to be there. I was showboating. Thankfully, in time and, unfortunately, due to some very loud wake-up calls, God changed my heart. I began slowly, committing to give 10 percent and then increasing that. I'll share more later in the book, but currently one of my goals is to live on the 90:10 principle: I want to give 90 percent of my income to God and use 10 percent to live on. We are not there right now; this is a lofty goal, but one that God can help us with eventually. It's God's money in the first place, but I'll admit, sometimes it's hard to remember that.

Now, does that mean we must drop everything and give all our money to God after reading this book? Maybe, but maybe not. It takes time to discover God's will. The point is, when you seek God and are truly surrendered to His will—that means being willing to do whatever He asks—you will have your motives in the right place. At that point, you will have reached the first major milestone on your journey toward fulfilling your purpose. The simple act of surrendering to whatever the Lord asks will actually allow you to hear His voice a whole lot more clearly.

A perfect example of this concept was displayed by my friends, Mike and Carol Hart. They're the founders of

ZOE House International, an organization that fights to free those trapped in the horrific world of human trafficking. Mike and Carol were living a very comfortable life of ease when God opened their eyes to the reality of human trafficking in Thailand. He called them to leave the security of their home and start an organization to rescue children from the slave trade in Southeast Asia. They immediately obeyed God's calling, and as a result, hundreds of children have already been rescued from brothels, dungeons, and horrendous factories. These children had no hope of rescue and were doomed to a life of sexual servitude or dismal slave labor. Because of Mike and Carol's obedience, they have now been given a second chance, are being rehabilitated, and have come to know a loving savior in Jesus Christ. What's more, ZOE has not only built children's homes, but they have expanded and opened ministry, vocational, language, and business schools as well to complete the rehabilitation process for these children. All this was possible because Mike and Carol answered the call. They were called to action. Imagine if, instead, they had sought to add an extra hundred grand to their retirement portfolio or wanted to "work toward" a new Mercedes. Hundreds of children would still be enslaved. Thank God, He called these two, and they obeyed. Now, countless children will be saved, both physically and spiritually. Praise God, from whom all blessings flow!

When Jesus calls you, change is inevitable. It may come slowly at first, and that is perfectly okay, but believe me—when you are saved, you are called, and when you are called, change is inevitable. Ask yourself: *Am I ready to make a change?* You can do it right now if you want to. Consider how you might begin to make even small changes. You could use your finances, your time, or even unused items around your house to honor God. The calling on each Christian's life is to go out and proclaim the kingdom of God, but there are many ways to accomplish that, and the call will look different for each of us. I believe the key is first checking and adjusting our motives and then being open to listen for His call and guidance. *God's call is your purpose.* He has given each of us abundant blessings, and it is our job and privilege to bless others in turn. Is it wrong to have nice things? No. Is it wrong to keep all of them for yourself? Without a doubt.

> Look at the birds of the air, for they neither sow nor reap nor gather into barns; yet your heavenly Father feeds them. Are you not of more value than they? (Matthew 6:26)

A concern for most is that when you surrender to the call of God, you may have to "live on the edge" in a life of lack and barely scraping by. Consider why we need what we think we need. Does God not say He even provides for the birds, although they don't sow or reap? Why, then, do we worry He'll fail to provide for us if we commit to serve Him? We only worry because of impure motives. If we're concerned that we may not keep up with the Joneses if we begin serving God, our motives are off-kilter. When we truly seek God, however, He will provide for every one of our needs as we serve Him and will do so in all circumstances. The difference is where He leads, He provides. God may allow our faith to be tested, but He will never forget us nor let us down. He may ask us to step out onto a lake in the middle of a storm or walk through a body of water that He promises to part as soon as the first step is taken, but He gives us these tests because He wants to witness the depth our faith.

One of the secrets to adjusting your motives is to remember life is short and eternity is…well, forever. Do you intend to gather treasures on earth or in heaven? What riches will you leave behind when your life on earth is over? We really need to begin these preparations now, and the good news is as we take the first step, it becomes easier. And as you continue being obedient, a remarkable thing begins to happen. You actually start to *enjoy* it!

Like most of us, I hate taxes. Signing a tax check can really ruin a great day, and if you read the Bible, it's evident people felt the same about taxes two thousand years ago. Jesus, however, commanded we pay Caesar what is Caesar's, so we are obedient, even though I think any sane person doesn't enjoy it. In contrast, however, how exciting is the thought of giving to God? Don't you want to be part of such an astonishing investment? Human souls are eternal and priceless, and when you support the kingdom of God, you are ultimately investing in the eternal salvation and restoration of human souls. This is why giving to God can be done with a tremendously joyful and gracious heart. As I have pondered these principles and have learned how to give more to the Lord, sometimes I truly get emotional when I think about the act of charity. This is really because it is God's money. We are truly privileged to steward the money God entrusted to us. When we understand the principles of giving to the kingdom of God, it's completely natural to get excited about this opportunity! God blesses us so much, and He gives us the chance to bless Him in return.

In 1 Timothy 6:17–18, Paul tells us:

> Command those who are rich in this present age not to be haughty, nor to trust in uncertain riches but in the living God, who gives us richly all things to enjoy. Let them do good, that they be rich in good works, ready to give, willing to share.

When I read this verse, I immediately think of Truett Cathy. Despite his success, he remained humble and always shared his wealth with those less fortunate, even when it was challenging for him economically. You may think, *I'm not a billionaire*, but if you live in a first-world country and live on more than ten dollars a day, you are in the elite 20 percent of the global population![2] That makes you rich, my friend, and subject to this commandment inspired by the Holy Spirit. Someday, I truly

---

1. Company Fact Sheet. Retrieved from http://m.chick-fil-a.com/Company/Highlights-Fact-Sheets
2. Shah, Anup. 2013, January 7. Poverty Facts and Stats. Retrieved from http://www.globalissues.org/article/26/poverty-facts-and-stats

hope others will look at my life and say, "Regardless of the situation, in the good times and bad, he honored God with everything he had." I believe that would be an epitaph worthy of a good legacy. What do you want your epitaph to say?

10

Sheep Are Dumb

When I watch football, I love watching Tom Brady play; he is as reliable as a Swiss banker, and he just gets the job done. He's the perfect quarterback to have in Fantasy Football. If it's fourth and one or the Super Bowl is on the line, I always want the ball in his hands. Tom remains calm at all times, and he never rants, hoots, or hollers. When he is in the huddle, you can tell his thoughts are collected and his behavior is even-tempered. Even if he is down by seven points with thirty seconds left on the clock, Tom walks onto the field with confidence, control, and the determination to win. Tom Brady's attitude and fortitude remind me of Jesus. Do you remember the story about the lost sheep in Luke 15:1–7? The passage reads:

> Then all the tax collectors and the sinners drew near to Him to hear Him. And the Pharisees and scribes complained, saying, "This Man receives sinners and eats with them." So He spoke this parable to them,

saying: "What man of you, having a hundred sheep, if he loses one of them, does not leave the ninety-nine in the wilderness and go after the one which is lost until he finds it? And when he has found it, he lays it on his shoulders, rejoicing. And when he comes home, he calls together his friends and neighbors, saying to them, 'Rejoice with me, for I have found my sheep which was lost!' I say to you that likewise there will be more joy in heaven over one sinner who repents than over ninety-nine just persons who need no repentance."

This situation must have been uncomfortable for the tax collectors and sinners. The Pharisees (religious leaders of the day) were watching them eat, making sure they followed the rituals of Jewish law strictly, and judging every move they made. If they didn't, the religious elite would whisper judgment upon them: how they don't belong and are inferior. I know how incredibly self-conscious I feel when I perceive judgment. I get nervous, which makes me angry, and I react differently than I would if I were at ease. You can relate, right?

Jesus however, remains calm, cool, and collected, and uses His words to reassure the known sinners and defuse the situation. He brings equality and compassion to the table. He compares those of us who have really strayed to lost sheep. Jesus reassures the sinners and chastises the Pharisees that God cares for His sheep, and no matter how many times we wander away, He will always search us out. Jesus shows in this passage that He is constantly searching for the lost. When He finds us, He puts us on His secure, strong shoulders and rejoices. There is no safer place, in all truth.

A major problem, however, is that sheep are dumb. They can hardly see, they have no upper teeth, and they can't defend themselves. If a wolf is preparing to attack, what do sheep do? They huddle together, bleating loudly with their faces in and butts out, waiting for the wolf to choose the plumpest option. Sheep are very dependent animals and were seemingly created to be led and taken care of. They are not fighters, and they're pretty defenseless without a shepherd. Sheep are dumb because, despite their vulnerabilities, they're always getting lost. They stray more easily than any other animal and frequently leave the safety of their flock. Sounds familiar, right? Humans are very much like sheep in this way. Jesus is the Good Shepherd, but despite His provision, best efforts, and faithfulness, we still stray. Thank God Jesus knows this and has prepared for it.

I think part of our problem is that, just like sheep, we often don't truly trust our Shepherd. If we did, we'd listen to Him when we knew we shouldn't be involved in something. No matter how green the grass on that cliff face looks, if we chase it, we could fall off the cliff. Our Shepherd knows this and time and time again, He comes after each one of us, to our rescue. What if we started to wise up a little? What if we began to nuzzle the leg of our Shepherd and spend time with Him? How much smarter would we become, spending some time with Him? This is God's will. Relationship. It's the only thing that moves us forward in our spirituality.

Many people believe that in the passage above, Jesus is talking only about an unsaved person accepting salvation. I believe in a sense it is, because all of us were created in God's image. The passage clearly talks about *sheep*, however, and this distinguishes the subjects from *goats*. Goat symbolism is typically used by Jesus to depict the unsaved of the world (Matthew 25:31–36). I believe this passage is talking about lost *sheep* (i.e., believers who have strayed). In fact, it may be talking about *you*. You see, Jesus is both defending His lost sheep, burdened by religious rituals, and also chastising the religious leaders. Yeah, sheep are dirty, but how can you save a sheep without touching it? (And why would you care if you love the sheep?) Of course, the elephant in the room was that the Pharisees were sheep themselves. They were dirty too, but in their denial of being dirty sheep, they wouldn't allow Jesus to rescue them. Instead, they judged the other sheep (sinners and tax collectors) and even judged Jesus as He rolled up His sleeves and rescued His dirty little flock. The sinners and tax collectors would enter heaven before the religious leaders for this reason.

"But what do you think? A man had two sons, and he came to the first and said, 'Son, go, work today in my vineyard.' He answered and said, 'I will not,' but afterward he regretted it and went. Then he came to the second and said likewise. And he answered and said, 'I go, sir,' but he did not go. Which of the two did the will of his father?"

They said to Him, "The first."

Jesus said to them, "Assuredly, I say to you that tax collectors and harlots enter the kingdom of God before you. For John came to you in the way of righteousness, and you did not believe him; but tax collectors and harlots believed him; and when you saw it, you did not afterward repent and believe him." (Matthew 21:28–32)

I once attended a service at a church in Saint Petersburg, Florida, and my friend nudged me and motioned to a young lady sitting in the row in front of us. I looked at him, puzzled, and he whispered she was one of the strippers from a club down the street from the church. Soon, the gossip spread like wildfire through the church, with people whispering, murmuring, and raising eyebrows about this woman. It really grieved me, and I wondered why we do this. Why weren't we happy for this woman's transformation? One of the lost sheep had been found, yet like Pharisees, all we could do was judge her for her past sins. Then I had to ask myself, "Who commits the greater sin: the woman who dances at a strip club or the man who watches her with lust in his heart?" They are both sinners, equal in the grief they cause to God's heart. I realized afterward that I should have asked how my friend how he would even know she was a stripper, but hindsight is always twenty-twenty.

When a sinner returns to God, a party is thrown in heaven. Isn't that astounding? They are dancing, singing, and celebrating because one sheep whom was lost has been found. Do you react that way when you find out that one of your friends or family members has become a follower of Christ? Or are you judgmental and wonder how long the change will last? I have been guilty of the latter, but I am now determined to have faith, rejoice in the future, and *be part of that person's continuing discipleship.* Too often, we sit back and judge others rather than rejoice with them when a change has finally been made.

I know God was most certainly elated when that woman walked into church that day, and I know if you have strayed, He will react the same way when you answer the Holy Spirit's calling. When you are lost, He will never on this earth give up His pursuit of you. Jesus will search for His lost sheep until they are found, and He will throw a huge party when you come back to Him! Jesus wants to call up His friends, bring out the strobe light, pump up the tunes, break out the rib eye steaks, and rejoice that you have come home. That's Christ's love. He is ready to make radical changes in your life if you let Him, but you have to answer His call. The Bible says He stands at the door of your heart and knocks. He will not force His way in, but when you are ready, He will be there with outstretched arms. He wants to bless you beyond your comprehension. He wants to help you in times of trouble and struggle. He wants to rescue you. He wants to give you everything you need so you can praise Him and show others how mighty this God of yours truly is. He wants to save you from judging others while you are in desperate need of rescue yourself. Being judgmental and having a false sense of righteousness are absolute killers to fulfilling God's purpose for your life. Humility is always the first step in going to God and as such, the message of this chapter is simple: if you are judging others, you most likely need rescue yourself. I pray that you and I can acknowledge this and return to a daily, disciplined relationship with Jesus.

Heaven will throw a party.

11

Superhero

In 2012, my brother and I went to a Seattle Seahawks game. The Seahawks were playing the New York Jets, whose star player was Tim Tebow. Now, my brother would undoubtedly be in the running for the planet's most devoted Tebow fan, so it's safe to say he only went to the game to watch his favorite player. In fact, my brother even believes he looks like Tim. (In reality, he's about four inches shorter and not nearly as muscular.) I humor him, though, nodding and smiling when he voices such delusions.

The game was played on the Seahawks' home turf in Seattle, but my brother, of course, sported his Tebow jersey proudly. For those unaware, Seahawks fans are notoriously loud and rowdy and proudly uphold the distinction of maintaining the "Loudest Outdoor Stadium." To add to the day's bad decisions, when my brother bought the tickets, he didn't realize he had chosen seats smack-dab in the middle of the "fan zone."

As we entered the stadium, the heckling started. By the time we reached our section, it was harassment. By the time we made it to our seats, I knew we were in for a long game. My brother was the only person wearing an emerald-green Tebow jersey in a sea of raucous Seahawks blue. Even if you live in Seattle and don't cheer for the Seahawks, you're at least smart enough to never attend the games. We weren't quite so bright.

My brother, of course, could not have cared less...at least at first. He believed it was entirely possible that Tim Tebow would spot his sore-thumb, green, number fifteen jersey in the sea of blue and run out to give him a high five or maybe a wink, and they would even exchange details. After the game, perhaps they'd walk off into the sunset as BFFs, and my brother would be greatly exalted for his courage on national TV. None of that happened.

The Seahawks dominated the game early. As the fans around us became increasingly drunk, they felt increasingly comfortable with sharing their true feelings about my brother and his Jets jersey. (Much to my brother's chagrin, and because I didn't have a death wish, I wore a Seahawks jersey. Also, Pete Carroll and Russell Wilson rule—go Hawks!) Eventually, the fans right behind us started calling my brother vulgar names and swearing at Tim Tebow. When the harassment reached a fever pitch, we decided it was time to take a break and hit up the concession stand. Things only escalated when we returned.

As we sat down, the guy next to me spat in our food. My brother and I are usually even-tempered people, but we aren't afraid of much in the world. The thought of facing sixty thousand belligerent fans, however, was a little more intimidation than we were used to. The more the fans drank, the more we approached physical violence. Eventually, my brother texted the stadium's security line, and to my relief, security guards came over and defused the situation. It was short lived, though, as the guards had to leave to attend to other business, and soon the craziness picked back up. I was caught between a state of fury and a legitimate fear of hospitalization. Soon, we felt so unsafe that we decided to pack it up and left the game early.

It would be great if the punch line of that story was my brother and I taking on two rows of angry Seahawks fans and somehow beating the daylights out of them in a superhero type of victory. It was real life, though, so we simply had to get out of there because we might truly have been killed. That didn't help me leave the anger behind. As we left, I couldn't stop thinking about the guy who spat in our food. I was enraged that a man could be so disrespectful. He didn't even know us! We were simply cheering for another team. As we walked up the stairs, ignoring the jeers and taunts, with every bit of my heart, I hated that man.

At the time, I truly wished I had a red-and gold-briefcase I could pop open, from which a super high-tech, artificially intelligent suit of weaponry would spring out and enshroud me. Then I'd teach that sick Seahawks fan a much-needed lesson in manners. Yep, it's no secret I love the Iron Man franchise. Deep down, I wish I were Tony Stark probably about as much as my brother wishes he were Tim Tebow. I even feel like I have some things in common with Tony Stark. As a type 1 diabetic, I carry a pump that provides insulin, necessary to keep me alive. Tony Stark is kept alive by an electromagnet in his chest. The similarities are uncanny really (kind of like my brother's similarities to Tim Tebow). There is really only one major difference between us: Tony Stark is actually a superhero. He teams up with other superheroes to save the world and preserve mankind. He sacrifices his health and safety for the good of others. What I wanted to do to the snack defiler was anything but heroic.

Here's the problem. Jesus, in my humble but educated opinion, is the master paradigm every superhero is modeled on. Jesus actually *did* step down from his Godhood to help mankind (Thor), lived His entire life sacrificially (just about all of the "good guys"), and ultimately sacrificed His life for us and was resurrected (Iron Man, Batman, Bucky Barnes, Captain Rogers…the list of copycat superheroes goes on). Jesus, however, gives us a commandment that seems to defy even these comic book heroes' logic. Instead of fighting people who make themselves our enemies, we are to *love* them.

"You have heard that it was said, 'You shall love your neighbor and hate your enemy.' But I say to you, love your enemies, bless those who curse you, do good to those who hate you, and pray for those who spitefully use you and persecute you, that you may be sons of your Father in heaven; for He makes His sun rise on the evil and on the good, and sends rain on the just and on the unjust. For if you love those who love you, what reward have you? Do not even the tax collectors do the same? And if you greet your brethren only, what do you do more than others? Do not even the tax collectors do so? Therefore you shall be perfect, just as your Father in heaven is perfect." (Matthew 5:43–48)

Oh man. That one is tough. Love our *enemies*? They are called *enemies* for a reason, after all. An enemy is someone we typically think it's okay to hate. We've all been there. I've said it more times than I'd like to admit. I've said it about strangers at football games, I've said it to my friends, and I've even said it to my family. *I hate that person.* Jesus didn't hate anyone. Guess what? If we call ourselves believers, we cannot hate a single person either. We can't have "frenemies" either. You see, contrary to this world's line of thinking, this is what makes Jesus the true superhero. Love. Jesus loves every single person in the human race and came to do battle with only spiritual powers of darkness and oppression. That is the context in which we have to see our "enemies." They behave as our enemies because they are lost and simply don't know any better.

> And when they had come to the place called Calvary, there they crucified Him, and the criminals, one on the right hand and the other on the left. Then

Jesus said, "Father, forgive them, for they do not know what they do." (Luke 23:33–34)

So how does all of this apply to your purpose and your calling? Well, the question is really, "How does it *not* apply?" If you really want to kick your purpose into high gear, start loving your enemies. There's a catch, of course. This process is not for the squeamish. First, you have to forgive them. That's the first step of love. That means wiping away any hope of recompense for injury they've done to you. It means I give that guy who spat in my food a free pass. No harm, no foul. I can't even think about whether or not he's a nasty human being. It doesn't matter because he doesn't know better. But what if someone had robbed me? What if someone had insulted my wife? What if someone harmed a member of my family? The more you escalate the offense, the trickier it gets. As I said, it's for the spiritually mature, yet the commandment is the same, no matter what. They were murdering Jesus. From the cross, He called for God to wipe that crime from their records. He calls us to the same path of *love*.

With all that said, it's always good to remember the "pros" of obedience however, as well as the "cons." When I would watch an *Iron Man* movie or *The Avengers*, I used to think: *Boy I wish I could do that! I wish I were a superhero.* After meditating on the scriptures above and giving it some thought, one day, I realized: *You can totally do that! You can be a Christian superhero.* Even in the fictional superhero universe, the protagonists usually face persecution and hatred despite their doing good. This is why a common theme is hiding their identity with a mask. Christ calls us to be bold and identify with Him. I should never wear a mask, but as a Christian, I can certainly help save someone's life. In fact, I could save many lives. I hold the key and knowledge that billions of people are searching for. I can do all of this simply by telling people about Jesus.

Sadly, instead, I often act as if I'm in a movie theater, watching life play out on a screen as I clutch my twenty-eight-dollar popcorn and diet soda. I observe, but I never act. If I simply hope that someone tells my unsaved friends and family about the love of Jesus while I sit idly and silently by, am I loving them? If Jesus calls us to love even our enemies, do you think we should be complacent toward our loved ones when it comes to knowledge of the most precious gift in the universe—namely, salvation? In superhero movies, good always triumphs over evil, but in life, there is no guarantee of the ending for everyone. That is the desperate truth Jesus is trying to get across to us.

The *Take Action* step in this chapter might even be the most critical piece of information in this entire book; God calls us to love and pray for *everyone*. This is our duty on earth—to serve others, to love others, and to share the gospel with others. Even our enemies. Jesus spells it out for us, plain and simple. In fact, He commands it. And to reinforce our theme of relationship, the best way to understand what Jesus wants from you is to read your Bible. What He asks, however, is straightforward: love people, put others ahead of yourself, honor and follow God in all things.

Of course, if you're anything like me, this is a lot easier said than done. I actually struggle most with the whole "love your neighbor" thing. I mean, I sometimes have the most trouble loving my literal neighbors. (In my defense, though, we really have had some doozies.) Take, for example, the retired couple who lived next to us in the first home my wife and I purchased. They really took the cake. At first, they seemed pleasant enough and were friendly, and all seemed in well in "Pleasantville." I soon became convinced, however, that they had installed cameras in our home. The husband was honestly the nosiest person I have ever met. He would constantly knock on our door and peek through our windows to check if we were home. He had zero respect for our privacy. Once, he held a meeting with some other neighbors in our parking space *on our property* regarding the state of our yard! The man frustrated me so often and so regularly that I said several times that I literally hated him.

We moved away after only a year and a half, and now that I have some distance from the situation, I am struck with a hard reality: I never once showed that man any love or shared the gospel with him, either in my words or my actions. I have to wonder if he even knew that I am a Christian. That's a harsh realization to reach. It's easy enough to say we should love our neighbors, but when push comes to shove and my neighbor turns out to be a real pain, can I follow through? How do we love the colleague who always takes credit for our work? How can we love the family member who never has a kind word to say? How can we love the so-called friend who spread lies about us? The answer is, "Start small." We may not have the strength to love, but God does. It takes faith. Everything God commands us to do requires faith. We have to take an action step and start small. But we have start. You never know when a small action will be an act of superheroism.

In 2012, my wife and I decided to take a road trip (and I mean a serious road trip, not just a drive to the next city). We drove from Los Angeles to Colorado and then to Utah, through North and South Dakota, and then Wyoming and beyond. Our goal at the time was to ultimately visit all fifty states. After this trip, I would have only six states to cross off my list. But, man, it was a lot of driving! We visited eight states in six days, and by visit, I mean crossed the border, took a picture, tagged ourselves on Facebook, and drove to the next state. The trip was a great time for us to connect, and we thoroughly enjoyed it, but by the end of the trip, we were tired, hungry, and just wanted to get home.

As we've come to expect in Los Angeles, as soon as we entered the city limits, we hit gridlock traffic. It was very frustrating to be exhausted and so close to home but stuck on the I-5, crawling at a snail's pace. I couldn't deal with it, so I decided to take my chances on State Route 14, and changed our route home. Just as we started making good headway, a massive truck, only several feet in front of us, suddenly careened across all four lanes of traffic and slammed into the concrete wall. He hit it with such force that the truck bounced off the barrier and lurched back across the freeway, smashing again into the left wall.

I instantly pulled onto the shoulder and ran over to help while Sara called 911. I looked inside to ask if the driver was okay but saw he was unconscious behind the wheel. The car was still revving, so I tried to pry the passenger-side door open, since the driver's side was jammed into the wall. My stomach dropped as I saw the dashboard was beginning to smoke. I reached through the smashed passenger window and managed to turn off the engine off so the car didn't catch fire, and I knew I had to get this guy out of the car. At that point, I realized no other drivers had stopped to help; Sara and I were the only ones.

What I saw next sickened me. People were slowing down to take pictures with their phones but then just kept driving on their way. I have never been so disgusted in all my life. I took a closer look at the driver, wondering how I was going to get him out alone, and noticed he was foaming at the mouth. I figured he'd had a seizure. By now, he was also covered in blood, and both of his arms were clearly broken. I had no idea what to do. I'm not a paramedic nor a doctor, and I've had no emergency medical training. Administering my daily insulin shot is almost more than I can bear.

As I stood frozen, terrified, and wondering how to help this poor man, I uttered a silent prayer: "God, please help us." Almost immediately, a car pulled over, and the driver told me she was a nurse and asked if I needed help. I enthusiastically said yes and accepted her assistance. Not a minute later, another car pulled over, and the man inside was a paramedic. The nurse said we had to remove the driver from the vehicle before he went into cardiac arrest, so I squeezed myself into the car and unbuckled him. We gently pulled him out of the truck's cab and laid him on the shoulder of the highway, but the man was still not responding. I heard the ambulance and the fire truck in the distance, but they were stuck in traffic. The nurse and the paramedic took over and had things under control, so I kept myself busy by directing traffic. People were rubbernecking, slowing down, eager to see what happened, while the traffic was preventing the fire truck and ambulance from arriving. After what seemed like an eternity (but was actually twenty-five long minutes), they arrived, tried to stabilize the man, and took him away. I have never been in a life-or-death situation like that before or since.

That day, the nurse, paramedic, and I were each faced with the same choice as everyone else on the road. Everyone was frustrated with traffic, tired, and just wanting to get home. We could have assumed someone else would stop and help, but the reality was that everyone was assuming that. I'm sure you know where I'm coming from with this story. It's easy to assume someone else will do the sacrificial work, but the reality is that everyone assumes that same thing. A few people realize this truth and sadly, it's a small percentage in the Body of Christ who do the heavy lifting.

I used to believe going to church was my only duty as a Christian. I'd get up early, put on my Sunday best, and drag myself to the service. I'd critique the worship set a little, think about where to go for lunch, and perhaps get hung up on a few notes the pastor made. It never really made a lasting impact on my life. If there was something I didn't like about the church, I could just choose another one. How often has this scenario played out for you? I'm not judging you; I'm getting to a point. How do we break this cycle? The answer is love. When we love humanity like Jesus loves them, it'll be a no-brainer to share the gospel. In fact, we won't have to stress about how to approach people or awkwardly try to bring up eternal life with a colleague at work. It will happen naturally in conversation or even merely by our example. Why? Because *love* will emanate from everything we do. People will be drawn to us, just as they were drawn to Jesus.

You really can be a superhero. In fact, Jesus calls you to the same path He walked Himself. He wants you to know deeply the sole importance of our purpose on this earth: to save the lost through the love of God. There really is nothing more important. And that should remove a lot of stress and pressure from you. Take action today and start understanding Christ's love by spending more time with Him. His nature will rub off on you and in turn, it'll affect everyone around. It's a great design, isn't it? But take that first step.

> "A new commandment I give to you, that you love one another; as I have loved you, that you also love one another. By this all will know that you are My disciples, if you have love for one another." (John 13:34–35)

12

The Easiest Way to Take Action Today

Have you ever had to cook dinner for a large group of people? At the writing of this chapter, I've just experienced a wonderful Thanksgiving with my family, and it always amazes me how much work goes into the meal preparation. Perhaps you've had to prepare a meal where it may not be quantity but quality instead? It might be a gourmet meal for someone special, famous, or even powerful? What if the president were to come over for dinner? Oh, imagine the stress! I'd bet you would ensure your home was absolutely spotless and maybe even hire a cleaning service? What kind of meal would you prepare? Would you be sneaky and hire a chef? How much planning and effort would go into that meal?

When I owned my restaurant in California, I once had to prepare a meal for over *four thousand* people. I didn't have Jesus physically present to multiply the food, so I knew this task would be no joke, and it turned out to be even more challenging than I'd imagined. I began planning months in advance: ordering, checking and double-checking, and calculating the amount of labor we needed, not to mention deciding what food to serve. We had to rent a U-Haul and a twenty-six-foot refrigerated truck just to transport everything to the location. In addition to utilizing my regular staff, we recruited over thirty volunteers to ensure everything went smoothly. I had never served a group that large before, so thorough preparation was imperative. Thank heavens it turned out to be a success.

Whenever I think about that event and what it felt like feeding an overwhelming and impossible number of people, I am reminded of when Jesus fed over five thousand people spontaneously. I was very concerned we wouldn't be able to serve our group successfully, so I have no doubt His disciples could relate. Matthew 14:13–21 reads:

> When Jesus heard it, He departed from there by boat to a deserted place by Himself. But when the multitudes heard it, they followed Him on foot from the cities. And when Jesus went out He saw a great multitude; and He was moved with compassion for them, and healed their sick. When it was evening, His disciples came to Him, saying, "This is a deserted place, and the hour is already late. Send the multitudes away, that they may go into the villages and buy themselves food."

> But Jesus said to them, "They do not need to go away. You give them something to eat."

And they said to Him, "We have here only five loaves and two fish."

He said, "Bring them here to Me." Then He commanded the multitudes to sit down on the grass. And He took the five loaves and the two fish, and looking up to heaven, He blessed and broke and gave the loaves to the disciples; and the disciples gave to the multitudes. So they all ate and were filled, and they took up twelve baskets full of the fragments that remained. Now those who had eaten were about five thousand men, besides women and children.

One thing that stood out to me is where the scripture says Jesus had compassion on the people and wanted to provide for them. I used to feel guilty when I read this because I would think about how many times I had quickly judged the homeless population that is so prevalent in Los Angeles. I would think things like: *What are they doing with their lives? They have to just be lazy. Why don't they just find any kind of job? If I can do it, they can do it.*

Of course, the reality is I have no idea what their circumstances are, and I'm in no position to judge. Jesus, however, who could judge us all, has unending compassion for these people. Many of the people I'm so quick to dismiss were likely the very ones drawn to Jesus that day near the lake. He did not avert his gaze nor ignore them, and what's even more fascinating is that right before this event, Jesus's beloved cousin,

John the Baptist, had just been murdered by King Herod and his wicked family. Jesus had actually withdrawn to get some quiet time to mourn and pray, yet He was still moved with compassion when the crowds sought His help.

Now Jesus, demonstrating His godhood yet again, decided to use the situation to teach His disciples as well. He simply told them to feed the crowd. Boy, I can only imagine how they felt, but I truly would not have envied their position. Feeding five thousand people requires tremendous strategic planning and preparation, neither of which the disciples had. But Jesus knew what He was doing. This was another of those "you of little faith" scenarios.

The disciples' experience reminds me of when I was a child; I sometimes had to tell my dad something I knew would disappoint him. It was difficult because I hated disappointing him; imagine how it must have felt to disappoint Jesus! (I know, we all likely disappoint Him often, but He still loves and cares for us.) The disciples, even though they protested a little, were most assuredly scrambling to accommodate Jesus's command. A small boy offered his lunch to the disciples: five loaves of bread and two fish. (Note this actually demonstrated a measure of faith, that they believed Jesus could use even a seemingly ridiculous portion of food.)

In those days, only men were counted at gatherings. The scripture records five thousand men gathered around Jesus, not to mention the women and children who came with the men. Still, through a creative miracle, Jesus provided enough food for everyone to eat their fill, and there were even twelve baskets of fragments left over. That blows my mind, and it should blow yours too. If those that witnessed the miracle didn't believe in God before, I am certain they did after the meal. There is no doubt in my mind the people started bowing down and worshiping Jesus.

So how does all of this relate to taking action toward fulfilling our purpose? Well, you might have noticed some of our themes popping up in the two stories above. Of course, there again is Jesus, the ultimate superhero, and the disciples were superheroes that day too. And of course, instead of getting annoyed with people, even when you're well within your rights to do so, you should strive to bless them. But this passage teaches us something more as well. It teaches us something highly profound *about* our purpose and, more importantly, how to take easy, immediate action toward either discovering or fulfilling your purpose this very day. Consider the following scripture:

What does it profit, my brethren, if someone says he has faith but does not have works? Can faith save him? If a brother or sister is naked and destitute of daily food, and one of you says to them, "Depart in peace, be warmed and filled," but you do not give them the things which are needed for the body, what does it profit? Thus also faith by itself, if it does not have works, is dead.

But someone will say, "You have faith, and I have works." Show me your faith without your works, and I will show you my faith by my works. You believe that there is one God. You do well. Even the demons believe—and tremble! But do you want to know, O foolish man, that faith without works is dead? Was not Abraham our father justified by works when he offered Isaac his son on the altar? Do you see that faith was working together with his works, and by works faith was made perfect? And the Scripture was fulfilled which says, "Abraham believed God, and it was accounted to him for righteousness." And he was called the friend of God. You see then that a man is justified by works, and not by faith only.

Likewise, was not Rahab the harlot also justified by works when she received the messengers and sent them out another way?

For as the body without the spirit is dead, so faith without works is dead also. (James 2:14–26)

Wow. *"For as the body without the spirit is dead, so faith without works is dead also."* Those are some deep words. James is essentially saying good works are the life source of your faith. Now for those unfamiliar with the weighty concept of grace, please know that we will never be *saved* by works. Good works, however, are absolutely a confirmation of one's faith. This concept may have just created a little spark of revelation in your spirit regarding your purpose. Here's what I mean: if you want the quickest, surest way to get started both discovering and fulfilling your purpose, begin with good works.

In a nutshell, I'm saying the perfect will of God for your life is something that has to be worked out in time. God has given every one of us specific gifts (Ephesians 4:8). We won't get into how to discover your gifts in this chapter, but know that you're good at something, and typically what frustrates you most about the world will reflect part of your purpose to help correct that. But to get started in discovering, refining, and developing your specific purpose, there is no better place to start than by helping people in need.

Some might argue that Jesus used a creative miracle to feed five thousand, while we are required to give of our possessions, but look a little closer. Jesus gave of something much more valuable than His possessions. His time of mourning. I'd say that trumps just about anything we can give, but we can start by helping homeless people with a meal, or filling a need for people from your church, or even helping your literal neighbor. Once you start obeying the command to help those in need, your gifts will begin to flourish, and God will create opportunities for your advancement and promotion in His kingdom, toward your ultimate calling. Believe me, this is how it works.

Again, following Jesus's example when He fed the five thousand, He preached the gospel to them before He fed them with physical food. Even though we all have various and unique gifts, everyone is called to (1) share the gospel with anyone and everyone we can (Luke 14:23), (2) help those in need, and (3) walk righteously before God. These are three things you can do every single day that will guarantee you rewards in heaven and will mature you in your calling and purpose right here on earth. In fact, the Apostle James defines pure religion as two of those three points:

> Pure and undefiled religion before God and the Father is this: to visit orphans and widows in their trouble, and to keep oneself unspotted from the world. (James 1:27)

Now, there is another element to this concept of helping those in need that will propel you even faster toward your destiny in God. In fact, it's critical, and if you don't practice this one habit, your efforts toward your good works will likely fizzle. It may not seem like a very "take-action" type of habit, but in order to consistently help those in need, we have to remain in an attitude of *thanksgiving* for what God has provided for us. Why? One reason is because thanksgiving generates compassion.

Thanksgiving automatically makes us aware of what we have, and when we become aware of what we have, we can clearly see how many others in the world have so much less. Trust me, thanksgiving will generate compassion, and we will immediately begin identifying what we can do or give to help others. Even if we have very little, whatever we can spare in our possessions or time to share with those who have even less will be seen and blessed by God.

"And whoever gives one of these little ones only a cup of cold water in the name of a disciple, assuredly, I say to you, he shall by no means lose his reward." (Matthew 10:42)

As we close this chapter, I want to ask: How seriously does God take helping those in need? Is it a suggestion? Is it a commandment? If we have a surplus of something, should we only bless friends and people at church or strangers too? (Surely not our enemies?) As always, when there is a documented event of Jesus setting an example, we can be sure God takes it very seriously. Consider the following statement by Jesus Himself:

"When the Son of Man comes in His glory, and all the holy angels with Him, then He will sit on the throne of His glory. All the nations will be gathered before Him, and He will separate them one from another, as a shepherd divides his sheep from the goats. And He will set the sheep on His right hand, but the goats on the left. Then the King will say to those on His right hand, 'Come, you blessed of My Father, inherit the kingdom prepared for you from the foundation of the world: for I was hungry and you gave Me food; I was thirsty and you gave Me drink; I was a stranger and you took Me in; I was naked and you clothed Me; I was sick and you visited Me; I was in prison and you came to Me.'

"Then the righteous will answer Him, saying, 'Lord, when did we see You hungry and feed You, or thirsty and give You drink? When did we see You a stranger and take You in, or naked and clothe You? Or when did we see You sick, or in prison, and come to You?' And the King will answer and say to them, 'Assuredly, I say to you, inasmuch as you did it to one of the least of these My brethren, you did it to Me.'" (Matthew 25:31–40)

That's a sobering scripture, isn't it? Jesus is placing the command to help those in the same context as the Great Judgment Day. In fact, it certainly appears He is saying a factor critical to eternal life is helping those in need. As we can see, God isn't playing games when it comes to taking care of our fellow man and woman. This is encouraging news, however, because it is so easy to begin fulfilling the call of God on your life. You can get started fulfilling your sense of divine purpose this very day. This very hour. Just begin helping someone in need, and you'll immediately experience a sense of joy no material possession on this earth can match. I believe that is how you get started, and then as your faith grows with your good works, God may even do the miraculous through *you*.

Do we need to experience the miraculous every day to experience this joy? Not at all. Even in Jesus's ministry, believe it or not, the miraculous was the exception rather than the rule. Jesus's primary purpose was to share the gospel with the world, and the miracles were to confirm His authority to present that gospel. I would argue, however, that we do in fact witness miracles every day, yet we often aren't thankful to God. Have you ever seen the miracle of birth? Whether it's a human or a kitten, it's mesmerizing. It's utterly miraculous. When we wake up, we know the sun will shine, purely by faith, and when we go to bed, we know the stars will appear. God does astonishing things each day, but because He hasn't fed five thousand people before our eyes *yet*, it's easy to forget the magnitude of His glory. I believe even something as simple as the money in your bank account is a gift from God. He provides for you each day in a variety of ways. If we make a conscious effort to see where He is working, I believe our lives would drastically change for the better.

In closing, I want to take a look at a scripture that unmistakably ties in the concepts of need, provision, and God's will:

In the meantime, His disciples urged Him, saying, "Rabbi, eat."

But He said to them, "I have food to eat of which you do not know."

Therefore the disciples said to one another, "Has anyone brought Him anything to eat?"

Jesus said to them, "My food is to do the will of Him who sent Me, and to finish His work. Do you not say, 'There are still four months and then comes the harvest'? Behold, I say to you, lift up your eyes and look at the fields, for they are already white for harvest! And he who reaps receives wages, and gathers fruit for eternal life, that both he who sows and he who reaps may rejoice together. For in this the saying is true: 'One sows and another reaps.' I sent you to reap that for which you have not labored; others have labored, and you have entered into their labors." (John 4:31–38)

That's quite a scripture isn't it? Jesus is saying explicitly that if we are doing our Father's will, we will be entirely fulfilled. In fact, Jesus called God's will His *food*. What He meant was that God's will nourishes us! It is a life-giving source of spiritual (and I would argue, even physical) nutrition.

To recap, how do we fulfill the will of God?

1. We become thankful to God for what we have.
2. We begin to help those in need—*anyone* we are able to help.
3. We walk righteously before God (do our best and quickly repent if we slip).
4. We begin to share the gospel of salvation with those we know need to hear it.

I don't think we'll find a much clearer path to begin taking action. Hopefully, you can see as well that it is a joy, not a burden. If you've tried to do any or all of these steps and it became a burden, you might have neglected doing it out of compassion and love for your fellow human being and out of love and relationship with your God. If so, please go back to the start and give it another try in that context.

When you've experienced the joy of sharing, the similarly profound concepts in the next chapter will already be a breeze for you.

13

Not from a Distance

Years ago, I knew a used car salesman who did little to discourage the stereotype. This man oozed charm and charisma, and he connected with people on a level that created implicit trust. Within five minutes of talking to this guy, you'd be sure of just about anything he told you. The man was also an outright liar. This salesman would tell his customers exactly what he knew they wanted to hear. The stories were always similar: regardless of which vehicle the buyer was looking at, the previous owner was a nonsmoking doctor's widow who had garaged the car and performed regular maintenance on it. After a while, enough cars were falling apart soon after purchase that folks began checking the title history. They'd discover the truth. Of course; it was never a sweet old lady who only drove it to bingo on Tuesday nights. This man was clearly not aware of Proverbs 5:21:

> For the ways of man are before the eyes of the Lord, And He ponders all his paths.

God watched this man and his shady dealings, and although he got away with a few sales at first, his business ultimately was not blessed.

I've mentioned I was heavily involved in my church as a teenager and my initial interest in attending was solely because of the pastor's daughter. Soon, however, I began to be inspired by the message. (God's ways are mysterious, I know.) One Sunday, my family, including my grandmother, attended a service with me. That particular morning, our pastor was teaching on finances and tithing. Granted, it was a powerful teaching and soundly based in the Word of God. It was so moving, in fact, that my grandmother decided she had to do something about it right then.

Now, my grandmother was sadly in the early stages of Alzheimer's, but truthfully, she's always been a little off her rocker, and a very hard life and years of alcoholism played a large factor. Experiencing the overwhelming urge to give, she stood up in the middle of the service and made her way to the front of the stage. (Note: this was not how our church collected the offering.) My grandmother could've waited for the basket to be passed around (oh, if only she could have) but instead, she walked straight up to my future father-in-law in the middle of the service and started pulling coins out of her purse and handing them to him. I almost died of embarrassment. *More power to you if you want to tithe, Grandma, but maybe a little discretion wouldn't kill us! I'm trying to make a good impression here.*

In Chapter Nine, we've already looked at the story Jesus told about another elderly lady giving into the offering (Mark 12:41–44). To recap, in the synagogues of that day, they had a large area where the people of Israel could bring their tithes and offerings. Rich people were walking up with much pomp and ceremony and, I imagine, taking as long as possible to unload their huge offerings into the container. They were clearly boasting and making a big deal of their giving so everyone could see how supposedly generous and righteous they were. Once their show was done, a poor, old widow approached the treasury and dropped in two little coins called *mites*. (The equivalent in modern currency would be somewhere around two dollars.) It was all the money she had in the world. She did not brag about it nor try to draw anyone's attention. In fact, she was probably embarrassed by her widowhood and by that being all she had to give. Thank God Jesus was watching her. He saw her heart and made note of its generosity. Instantly, He called out to all the worshipers, including the boastful rich, and proclaimed (paraphrased), "This woman is giving more than any of you rich people! You gave a fraction out of your wealth, but she gave everything she had."

The reason I repeated this story is because I want to reiterate that Jesus measured what she gave by what she *held back*.

Similarly, my grandmother didn't have much money, but she had no hesitation (I mean zero) to get up and give whatever she had on her at the moment. At the time, I didn't see her generosity so clearly. I was embarrassed and was sure I'd have to find another church and possibly even move out of the state. I knew I'd never get to date the cute girl. With a new perspective, however, I am deeply touched by her gesture. So what did my grandmother understand then that I didn't? I believe she understood the Lord was watching not only what she withheld but how long it took her to give. He was watching, just as He watched that poor widow in the synagogue, just as He watched that used car salesman.

So what does that mean for us as believers (and even our nonbelieving readers)? For the Christian, the Holy Spirit resides inside of you. The Spirit of Jesus Christ has made His home within your spirit, and you are never alone. For the nonbeliever, the Holy Spirit also resides on this earth and speaks to your conscience (John 16:7–8). Besides God the Father and Jesus being able to see all we do from heaven, we have God (the Holy Spirit) right here with us every day. He sees all and experiences all we do as Christians.

Wow! Does that make you reconsider some of your actions? How you drive, how you speak, or how you respond when you are angry? What about how you behave around the opposite sex or when you want to deduct something you know isn't really business-related from your taxes? I know when I realized this, it definitely made me think twice about all I do.

Of course, there are two sides to that coin. On one hand, we can think of God watching us as "being under a perpetual spotlight." Kind of like "Big Brother." Who needs that, right? On the other hand, however, it means His love, power, and security are just as available. The difference is our heart's attitude. Both the poor widow and the rich people knew they were being watched. The rich put on a show, thinking they weren't being watched *all the time*. The widow gave, knowing that her life was in God's hands anyway, and if she starved, she'd soon be in heaven with her Creator. (Instead, her righteousness is still used as an illustration two thousand years later as a memorial.)

You see, the fact that God is always watching is a tremendous benefit to us. Once we get over our denial that our lives have always been naked before Him anyway, we can actually begin to understand He's *always* there to help. In this context, consider Him like a parent helping a child ride a bicycle without the security of training wheels for the first time. Perhaps your mom or dad ran behind you while you were learning, and perhaps you've run behind your child as he or she tries to maintain balance. Your parents were there to catch you, and you were there to catch your child. God is the same way. Doesn't that perspective take some of the pressure off?

When I was younger, though, I'll admit I felt so awkward when the offering basket was passed around. Everyone watched to see who contributed and how much. Sometimes, I would give, and other times, I wouldn't. When I did contribute, did I give with a cheerful and generous heart or out of guilt and duty? I don't remember, but I am sure that more often than not, it was actually out of peer pressure and sheer obligation. That's not God's plan for us. He wants us to simply be transparent before Him, weighing up what He has done for us and considering what we might offer Him. In contrast, though, I believe most of us are in bondage to a warped sense of what's fair. We're habitual scorekeepers, diligently ensuring we're never taken advantage of. The inherent problem with scorekeeping, of course, is we have a deep-seated cognitive bias. We tend to place more weight on what we give rather than on what we receive.

To be perfectly honest, this has been one of the biggest struggles in my marriage. I love my wife so much because she's such a strong follower of Christ and wants to so wholly obey Him. Sara is devoted to the Lord and consequently gives gladly with a full heart. I, on the other hand, have historically had a far more difficult time giving money away and an even harder time doing so joyfully. I can follow God's commandment to give, but it is not always with the most willing heart. I have often forgotten it is all God's money anyway. He has given it, and although He doesn't want to, He would be well within His rights to take it away if He so chose.

Here's the point: God is not just watching what we give. He's watching what we hold back. I believe understanding this concept is directly related to *how* we give. What do I mean? When we understand God is the parent behind us on our first ride on the bicycle, we believe He'll never allow us to beg for scraps of bread after we've given generously to others. I know this shift in mind-set is tough. That's the challenge. We're still on the overarching topic of *Taking Action*, and in fact, grasping this concept is a key that will completely unlock the previous chapter for you.

Let me ask you: Do you worry about how you are going to pay the grocery bill while knowing that you are also supposed to tithe? Do you think about all the other things you could buy with that money rather than giving it to the church? Maybe you wrestle with the idea of skipping a week, or perhaps you're hesitant to give because you don't have full trust in how your church will spend your contribution? These are arguments that plague families every week. I know because we've experienced them. At the end of the day, however, while I believe we are supposed to be wise in where we give, we can't use these questions as excuses to *not give*. That would be withholding more than we should and, to be honest, the money already belongs to God; when it doesn't make it to Him, we are actually stealing. Yes, I know this is getting a little heavy, but I also need to tell you the truth, which has two sides.

Now, for that key to unlock the last chapter. Remember, we discussed how to fulfill the will of God in your life, with the first of four milestones being that we're thankful to God for what we have? This chapter is the key to that first step, which, I believe, in turn unlocks all of the subsequent steps.

When we understand and accept that our hearts, intentions, and motives are essentially naked before God, we typically (like children) point the finger back, and ask, "Well what have YOU done for me lately, Lord?"

Yeah, we've established that He sees your heart, so He knows you're thinking it. Don't stress; He's a loving God. But let's go ahead and ask ourselves what has He done for us lately? The truth is, outside of that one little detail of being tortured and dying in our places, we really have no idea just how much He does for us every day. You are still here on this planet, so I'm guessing you aren't starving to death, and if you live in the West, you're probably in the richest 5 percent of the *entire world*. I think if we saw how much He really protects us from each day, we'd lose our minds. Seriously.

The truth is that what He does for us *far* outshines anything we could ever do for Him. You see, if He's watching what we hold back, it's because He desires for us to be greater conduits of His blessings. No, I'm not talking about giving *to* receive. I'm saying that it's a spiritual law that you sow what you reap, and if you're sowing generosity, you're going to reap generosity. The more God can trust you with, the more He'll expand your vision. And where He guides, He provides. He's not watching you *expecting* you to hold back more than you should. He's eagerly expecting you to do well, so He can trust you to give more.

Recently, I was listening to a pastor discuss this very subject, and I had an epiphany. He approached the topic differently to anything I'd ever heard. He asked the congregation why we seem so somber when the offering bags are passed. "Receiving offering is a celebration," he said. "An opportunity to serve the Lord and make Him smile." He then challenged us: from that day forward, when the offering bags were passed, we were to cheer, clap, and whistle because we had the chance to give Jesus just a small amount of what He has already given us. That day, as the ushers passed around the offering after the sermon, everyone cheered, clapped, hooted, and hollered! It was a little strange at first, but as we kept doing it week after week, I realized our pastor was exactly right. It is a simple way to bless God, and it's an effective way to change our attitude. God has also promised that in return, He will bless us again.

So if this speaks to you and you've been struggling with guilt, thanklessness, or giving as you should, I urge you to make the simple adjustment in your heart right now and take action to hold back less when you give this week. The next week, hold back a little less, and so on. Pretty soon, you will be so astounded at the lives you're changing and how blessed you are that you'll wonder why you weren't doing this sooner.

14

Loopholes and the Wisdom of Jesus

would make a terrible poker player. You see, I have a very visible tell (a sudden change in behavior that pops up any time I am nervous), and if you know what to look for, it will always give me away. My wife knows my tell. Boy, does she know it. If she asks me a question and I am not telling the whole truth and nothing but the truth, I'll involuntarily give a little smirk. That darn smirk gives me away every time.

"Honey, did you take the dog out?" she'll ask.

"Uh, yeah, he's been out." *At least, he's been out this morning* (smirk).

Sara always knows, and I'm always busted.

We've all had to answer "yes" or "no" questions. Maybe when you were a kid, some classmates tried to trick you into revealing you still slept in your parents' room when you had a bad dream. Did you answer yes or no? Perhaps your boss asked if you had completed that assignment. You were almost done, but you couldn't totally wrap because you were helping your colleague troubleshoot *their* part of the assignment. Do you answer yes or no? Or maybe a nonbeliever asks if you truly believe in God despite all the mayhem and evil in the world. You can't answer "maybe" to questions like these. It can become very difficult when you're asked a question that has more serious implications, which leaves you no alternative but to shoot straight, tell the complete truth, and bear the consequences. Jesus faced such a situation.

As I mentioned before, I don't believe anyone in the history of life has enjoyed paying taxes. Imagine for a moment how difficult it would be to pay taxes to the president of a foreign country that was occupying yours while his soldiers were treating your people like dogs. In the Gospel of Luke, we see men sent by Israel's religious leaders to try to trap Jesus. They thought they had a foolproof snare either to catch Him giving advice that was contrary to Roman law or to seemingly ally Himself with Rome:

> So they watched Him, and sent spies who pretended to be righteous, that they might seize on His words, in order to deliver Him to the power and the authority of the governor.

> Then they asked Him, saying, "Teacher, we know that You say and teach rightly, and You do not show personal favoritism, but teach the way of God in truth:

Is it lawful for us to pay taxes to Caesar or not?" (Luke 20:20–22)

These men asked a question that was designed purely to get Jesus in trouble with either the Roman rulers or the townspeople. The people despised paying taxes to Caesar, but Jesus could not honestly tell them they didn't have to pay. That would have gone against the laws of Caesar and consequently against God's laws, too. It was an overt attempt to trap Jesus under the guise of a pious question.

The first thing to understand is despite their seemingly humble words, these men's hearts were evil. With even a casual analysis, we can see they knew Jesus was righteous and would not instruct people to break the law. These falsely pious men were trying to use Jesus's righteousness against Him. As we can see, they hated the fact that the average man and woman in the street deeply loved Jesus. They were envious and wanted to discredit Him despite His godly works. Jesus, of course, faced a genuine challenge: He couldn't tell the people not to pay taxes, because (astoundingly to some of us) the ruling authorities represent God's authority, as we can see in Romans 13:1–7:

Let every soul be subject to the governing authorities. For there is no authority except from God, and the authorities that exist are appointed by God. Therefore whoever resists the authority resists the ordinance of God, and those who resist will bring judgment on themselves. For rulers are not a terror to good works, but to evil. Do you want to be unafraid of the authority? Do what is good, and you will have praise from the same. For he is God's minister to you for good. But if you do evil, be afraid; for he does not bear the sword in vain; for he is God's minister, an avenger to execute wrath on him who practices evil. Therefore you must be subject, not only because of wrath but also for conscience's sake. For because of this you also pay taxes, for they are God's ministers attending continually to this very thing. Render therefore to all their due: taxes to whom taxes are due, customs to whom customs, fear to whom fear, honor to whom honor.

I just love this account of Jesus being tested, because in it we see His wisdom being far greater than even Solomon's, from whom ancient world leaders traveled far and wide to get counsel. While we might think this was a real dilemma, Jesus probably smiled when He answered these hypocrites as only the son of God can:

> But He perceived their craftiness, and said to them, "Why do you test Me? Show Me a denarius. Whose image and inscription does it have?"

> They answered and said, "Caesar's."

And He said to them, "Render therefore to Caesar the things that are Caesar's, and to God the things that are God's."

But they could not catch Him in His words in the presence of the people. And they marveled at His answer and kept silent. (Luke 20:23–26)

Wow. He told them to give to Caesar what was Caesar's and to God what is God's! Jesus not only solved a tricky riddle, He did so with advice for these corrupt men: *give to God what is God's*. I believe He meant our hearts. Our hearts should always belong to God. If we seek to fulfill our own desires, we are not giving God what we rightfully should. We are shortchanging Him of His due. He created us, and withholding our hearts (i.e., our obedience, love, and devotion) from Him is nothing short of sin. These men failed to recognize Jesus as the son of God because they had withheld from God what was duly His.

The crowd marveled because of Jesus's wisdom, and those hypocritical men quickly shut their mouths and shrank into the shadows. How did Jesus have such seemingly spontaneous wisdom? Easy. His heart is pure (I speak in the present tense because He is risen, alive, and very active). The answer was obvious to Jesus because He spent time with His Father in prayer (i.e., relationship). He also knew the Word of God. It was a no-brainer that not only should we be obedient to the ruling authorities, but that there is a huge difference between what we give to worldly authorities and what we should give to God.

But, honestly, aren't we just like those corrupt men? How often do we try to find loopholes in the Word or a way out of obeying God's commandments? *I can have church at home watching a service on TV, and it's the same as "not forsaking the assembling of ourselves together."* (Hebrews 10:25) Or *I'm a man, I'm hardwired to stare at attractive women*, while Jesus said to lust after a woman is the same as adultery (Matthew 5:28). Looking for loopholes is the same sin. It boils down to dishonesty and maybe even a bit of rebellion. In Deuteronomy 6:16, the Word says to not test God. I don't want to go so far as to point fingers, but just to introduce the idea of even white lies and little challenges to God's sovereignty is completely sinful.

So where I am going with all of this? Well, just like the townspeople in Luke's Gospel, we still hate paying taxes, and I would even say many of us look for loopholes, not only in paying taxes but also in God's commandments. Not much has changed, but the same rule firmly still applies: we must follow what the Bible teaches, and that means paying taxes and giving to God what is God's. There's no "maybe" about it. What does God desire? Your heart. Earlier, in Luke 10:27, Jesus spells it out unmistakably:

So he answered and said, "You shall love the Lord your God with all your heart, with all your soul, with all your strength, and with all your mind, and your neighbor as yourself."

Obedience to give God what He is due is a condition of the heart, and giving our hearts continually to God is what Jesus is really commanding us to do here. It's no mystery how we do that: we simply *take daily action* toward an increasingly deeper relationship with Him. When we do this, tithing, loving our neighbor, and obedience to God will become a joy and a breeze. We won't have to look for loopholes. It all starts with the heart, though. I urge you today to search your heart and see if there is any rebellion in there, no matter how slight. Don't be ashamed, because God can and will set you free. But you have to go to Him in humility and with an open heart. It is always far more rewarding to simply obey God as quickly as possible, as the scripture below shows us:

So Samuel said: "Has the Lord as great delight in burnt offerings and sacrifices,

As in obeying the voice of the Lord? Behold, to obey is better than sacrifice, And to heed than the fat of rams." (1 Samuel 15:22)

As you continue to take action toward your purpose by purifying your heart, your results will increase exponentially. The thing is, you need to have your heart pure before you can truly hear what God is calling you to. As you'll see in the next chapter, God has a very specific plan for your life, and one day you will likely come face to face with a decision to answer yes or no to a life-changing question from God. Will you be prepared?

15

The Most Important Action We Can Take

I once heard a pastor tell of an event that happened to him a few years ago. He was out of town for a conference, and in his hotel room one night, he had an extremely vivid dream. He was about to fly home to California the next day, and in the dream, he was aboard that same flight. While the plane was in the air, everyone heard a deafening bang followed by a loud crash. Suddenly, the plane began falling from the sky, with no engine power.

In his dream, his first reaction was to unbuckle his seat-belt, jump out of his seat, and start to preach the gospel of Jesus. He figured if he were going to die, there was no time for embarrassment, and he might as well take whomever he could with him to heaven in their last seconds. As he preached salvation to the passengers, some yelled at him to shut up, while others screamed in terror, "Yes! I want to give my life to God!" Suddenly, he woke up and realized it had only been a dream. The lifelike dream deeply affected him, though, and he wondered if it was a warning of some kind.

The next day, he had to board that plane and fly home. Would you get on that plane without pause? I'll be very frank and say I would be hesitant to say the least. I'd think, "No thanks, I'll just wait for another plane or take a train, or maybe I'll just walk back to California." I personally would have done just about anything to avoid getting on the plane I'd dreamed about. But that wasn't what this man did. Instead, he called his wife and told her about the dream. He said in the event the plane went down and God wanted to use him to save a few souls on that plane (by the skin of their noses), she should know the story. He wanted her to know his life wasn't a waste because he died for Jesus. Naturally, his wife was upset, but what could she do? Her husband was completely sold out to his King, and words can't describe how much she respected him for it.

That day, the man boarded the plane, and all the passengers shuffled in and jammed their luggage into the overhead bins, and finally everyone had taken their seats. At the head of each aisle, a flight attendant went through the mandatory emergency drills while nobody really paid attention. Except the pastor, of course. Soon, the plane taxied out onto the runway and accelerated. Faster and faster the scenery whizzed by, until the front wheels began to lift. The plane shuddered and shook, but in a moment, they had lifted off smoothly without incident. The pilot increased the throttle, and the plane began to climb and climb toward the clouds. Suddenly, as they reached cruising altitude, there was a loud POP! from the back of the plane. The pastor jumped up out of his seat, raised his hands and was about to start preaching the gospel. As he stood there, a startled passenger waved over to him from the back of the plane and called out that he had inflated balloons from Disney World in his luggage that he'd "forgotten" to remove before boarding. The change in altitude and pressure had burst the balloon. Slowly realizing they were not about to die in a fiery crash after all, the man slumped back down in his seat, almost disappointed he didn't get the chance to preach the gospel on his way out of this world.

What strikes me most about this story is that many of us will do extraordinary things when our lives are on the line. We will beg, we will cry, we will fight to the very end, won't we? I love that this pastor was half-expecting a disaster but still submitted himself to board that plane. When he heard the pop, he didn't hesitate; he knew exactly what he had to do, and he did it. That's complete obedience to God, my friends. That can only happen when you've been seeking and practicing God's plan for your life for so long that your motivations are completely submitted to Him. That's an advanced level of faith, which will most clearly reveal God's purpose in your life. In fact, this story makes me think of when Abraham was about to sacrifice his only son, in obedience to God. Bear in mind, Isaac was the son born of a promise that had taken decades to fulfill and was supposed to be the one on whom God would build the promise of a great nation, as He had told Abraham:

Then they came to the place of which God had told him. And Abraham built an altar there and placed the wood in order; and he bound Isaac his son and laid him on the altar, upon the wood. And Abraham stretched out his hand and took the knife to slay his son.

But the Angel of the Lord called to him from heaven and said, "Abraham, Abraham!"

So he said, "Here I am."

And He said, "Do not lay your hand on the lad, or do anything to him; for now I know that you fear God, since you have not withheld your son, your only son, from Me." (Genesis 22:9–12)

God definitely tests us. The scripture says He'll never test us with evil, but without a doubt, He wants to see what is in our hearts. I believe in the same way Abraham passed this test, showing he feared God, and was willing to trust God with the most precious thing he had. The pastor on the plane passed the same test. I love both stories because they were so readily willing to do what God asked. He knew he had a job to do, and he did it. He was willing to get on a plane that might go down in order to reach even one soul for the gospel. What an awesome story, and what an awesome man of God who could have such a terrifying vision and still be obedient knowing he might die doing God's will.

What's interesting is that the first time I heard that sermon, I was getting ready to board a flight to Florida. The plane was huge, with nearly every seat taken, and as we took off, I thought about that pastor's story. The plane taxied out and took off, and we climbed and climbed. The dull roar of the plane's engines drowned out all other noise as we accelerated to cruising altitude above the clouds. Suddenly, the plane shook and dipped. A few people around me gasped, while the sermon I'd just heard rang in my ears. Again, the plane dipped and shuddered as it were buffeted by a severe pocket of turbulence. The seat belt signs dinged in seeming distress, and the captain's voice squawked across the intercom that we were experiencing turbulence and to please remain in our seats and buckle our seat belts. The entire scene was like something out of a nightmare.

Instantly, I found myself thinking, "If this plane goes down, what would be my first reaction? What would I do if we started to fall from the sky? Would I jump out of my seat and start preaching? Or would I scream, holler, and pray for myself? Could I honestly say I would reach out to the person next to me with the gospel?" As these thoughts raced through my mind, the turbulence dissipated. I turned to carefully look at the strangers sitting around me and realized I had absolutely no idea when their lives would end. Was this my opportunity to reach out and talk to them? Had anyone ever shared the gospel with them?

That moment was a wake-up call to me. I came face to face with the question of whether or not I would take the greatest action of all when the opportunity arose. Maybe I would have preached if the plane went down; maybe I would have been too distracted by fear. More importantly, I realized that someday we will all die. I guarantee it. It is appointed to each man and woman to die once (Hebrews 9:27). If you believe in eternal life through Jesus and eternal death by separation from Him, just reduce the timeline from "someday" to possibly today. Or possibly tomorrow. Possibly in eighty years. What I am saying is that when you simply remove the "someday" factor, it clarifies your ultimate purpose perfectly. If you and your loved ones had just one day left on this planet and you knew they did not believe in Jesus Christ, do you think you would do anything and everything to persuade them?

Instead, do we miss the opportunities God gives us because we are waiting for something catastrophic to happen? The shift that needs to take place in our minds is understanding that it's not for us to choose when we feel comfortable sharing the gospel with someone. We simply don't know when it will be too late. Too often, we worry we may look weird or be rejected if we try to share the gospel. I'd much rather be labeled a weirdo before man than an unfaithful servant before

Christ. You just never know what God is going to put before you or what He may call you to do.

People in the area where I lived in California often told me they felt called to live in that beautiful community, but I find myself wondering if that's really true. You see, I remember saying that very thing as a young businessman, trying to get my first restaurant. I too would comment on how great our community was and how I truly felt God was calling me to my community for this reason or that. Realistically, I look back and can see I didn't have much of a basis for my beliefs, other than trying to convince myself my plans were in line with God's because my surroundings were prestigious and comfortable. After many years, I believe I am homing in what God's *revealed individual* will is for my life, but that's only after I submitted myself to do whatever He asked of me.

In this final chapter of the section, I want to really get the point across that there is no greater action you can take than to go out and reach people—to share the gospel of Jesus Christ. At its most refined, *that* is your purpose. *That* is what you are called to do. Although God has promised to provide for you in your service to Him, don't get it back to front; you are not called to have a comfortable life, nice clothes, or fancy dinners. We are *all* called to reach and preach, nothing more. How we individually go about it is God's exciting revealed will for our personal lives, but our primary purpose will never change this side of heaven. That makes everything a lot easier. You can start where you are today simply by committing to be obedient to whatever God asks of you. You'll know when it's Him.

Ask yourself if you are willing to put yourself and your comfort on the line. Whether it be standing up in a plane and preaching or missional living in an underprivileged community that needs to be changed from the inside out. Are you willing to pack up and go wherever He calls you? Let's say God is calling you to your community; what are you doing to answer that call? Have you prepared your heart to do whatever God asks of you in your community? Could you be labeled a pariah for the name of Jesus? Or perhaps He has placed it in your heart to work in ministry abroad or in another state or province? Are you being obedient? Because the greatest action you can ever take toward your purpose is starting where you are now and being willing to do whatever God asks to save souls. The good thing is that even though it may initially test you, it will always, always, *always* be good and promote you in His kingdom in the long run.

If you can pass that test, you could very well be ready for the next level.

Section 3

Finding Your Calling

In this final section of the book, we circle back round to the beginning again and take a closer look at the theme of *purpose*. I pray that in the last two sections you were awoken to the fact that without understanding your God-given purpose, you were missing out the deep treasures God has prepared for you. Once you awoke to that truth, you (hopefully) were able to refocus your life and begin taking action steps toward your purpose.

Finding Your Calling is the third theme of the book. In this section, you'll begin to understand what it means to be a mature believer and discover the deeper rewards that are associated. By answering God's calling, you become an increasingly obedient disciple of God, and as a result, you become an increasingly brighter light to the world. Your life will become one that will be noticed and desired by others, just as your Master's is before you. You will have a life filled with challenges but even more deeply filled with God's joy and peace. You will live the highly fulfilled life you've always longed for—a fulfill-ment you will never receive from this world. By choosing to follow God's plan for your life, you will find the satisfaction you deeply long for.

Let's get started.

16

You're Called for a Specific Purpose

Did you know that you're not reading this book by accident? In fact, it is my belief God had a very specific plan to lead you right to this very point, right now. Every day, the Holy Spirit is speaking to everyone in the world, both believers and nonbelievers, and in seeking to find your God-given purpose, you have heeded His voice. Everything in your past, all of your decisions, all of your mistakes, and all of your successes have culminated in this moment. I'm not saying reading this book is the culmination of your life's aspirations, but this moment and the next are no surprise to God. And I would say the fact that you're reading a book about purpose and calling is definitely no accident. You've simply taken the first step in obeying God's calling.

Many times, I believe we're so hard on ourselves that we think events in our past will always hinder us. That notion is far from the truth. God is constantly leading you, sometimes whether you realize it or not, and He will always help you redeem (buy back or make up) the time in a way that only He can. So just trust Him. The Holy Spirit is speaking to you because

He wants to lead you to discover your very *specific* purpose, and you're right on the brink of discovering it.

The greatest thing God did was send His Son to earth, and to understand the rest of this chapter, you must grasp that Jesus was sent in a very specific way, for a very specific purpose. In Bethlehem, on the night Jesus was born, there was nowhere for His mother to give birth. Because the Roman Caesar Augustus had decreed that all of the Roman Empire be taxed, all of the surrounding region was traveling to Bethlehem to pay their taxes and register in a census. Jesus's parents were likely traveling more slowly because Mary was due to give birth at any time, and as a result, by the time they reached Bethlehem, all the inns, hotels, and bed-and-breakfasts were completely full. I'm sure Mary was not too pleased to take such a long journey, likely on the back of a donkey, when she was due any day, not to mention how much Joseph had to have been stressing. When they inquired at the last inn, the innkeeper told them he had no vacancies, but he said if they were truly desperate, they could sleep in the inn's barn with the animals. The dirty, smelly animals. Having no other options, they had to take it.

Imagine that scenario for a moment. Mary is nine months pregnant. She and Joseph have been visited by an angel and told she is carrying the Son of God. She's traveled about ninety miles, about a four-day journey on an uncomfortable donkey, to pay *extra* taxes decreed by a foreign government. And she begins to go into labor. If anyone ever had reason to question God's purpose for her life, it was Mary. Regardless, God had a very *specific* purpose.

In the middle of the night, Mary's water broke, and Jesus was born in a barn that reeked of manure, and the Son of almighty God was placed on a bed of straw in a feeding trough (the less glamorous word for *manger*). If you were in charge of how God's Son was going to be brought into this world, I'm sure at the very least you would have booked a suite at a five-star hotel, ordered the finest blankets and sheets, and purchased the most decadent crib and stroller. But God's ways are not our ways, and He most definitely had something different in mind.

Make no mistake, God intended for Jesus to be born in a humble shack where animals were kept. That should tell you something about God's priorities. He doesn't care about the material things we have nor the preparations we make; He cares about what's in our hearts. We might think that it was a mistake for Jesus to be born in a feeding trough, but God planned Jesus's birth at exactly the right time and in exactly the right place. In Micah 5:2, it was even prophesied Jesus would be born in lowly Bethlehem:

> But you, Bethlehem Ephrathah,
> Though you are little among the thousands of Judah,
> Yet out of you shall come forth to Me
> The One to be Ruler in Israel,
> Whose goings forth are from of old,
> From everlasting.

We may be stressed about where we have been, where we are, or where we are going, but we need to trust that God knows exactly what is going on in our lives and that He still has a plan for us. As fallen people working toward growth in the Lord, however, it can be pretty easy to lose sight of the fact that God is still in control and that He has a master plan. We become tired and lose our focus due to the daily cares of this life. To add to that, our enemy, Satan, is always lurking, trying to tempt us to take the bait, which he's always hoping leads to a fall. Satan is cunning; he tempts us and then tries to condemn us for giving him the time of day. He whispers in our ears, trying to dredge up our failures and past sins, and tells us we will never move past nor overcome them. He would like nothing more than to have us believe we are worthless disappointments and we are so far out of the plan of God that we are irrecoverable. Or worse, if we even start now, we'll only fulfill a small portion of what God had planned for us. This is a tremendous lie, but one that ironically, can keep you in a state of indecision and complacency. Worse, it can also have you believing God's calling is something magical that may someday reveal itself to you. With these distractions, it is possible to be delayed in fulfilling the call of God.

To explain my point, consider the following analogy: have you ever been waiting on a phone call you couldn't wait to answer? As a teenager, I couldn't wait for Sara to call me. I was so excited she might want to share the news of her day that when I went to bed, I would rest my old Nextel phone on my chest, hoping its vibration would wake me up if she called. Most of the time, she didn't call, or worse, I'd wake up and find I'd rolled over and missed her call. I would immediately call Sara back, but by then, she wouldn't answer. She'd always claim she was busy or didn't hear my call, but I believed she was trying to teach me a lesson. (Isn't that true of all women?)

In a similar (though less humorous) way, God calls us with very specific instructions but often, we're either "sleeping" or so distracted that we don't hear the call. One reason might be because we weren't staying close to God. Worse, though, maybe we've heard the call and are ignoring it out of fear. I personally did this for years! We do this because we know what He is calling us to takes us out of our comfort zone. We metaphorically let the phone ring even when we know whom it is, afraid to answer.

At the age of sixteen, I felt God's calling in a powerful way. I knew He was calling me to preach the gospel, but I was very afraid. I doubted I had the talent or the ability to lead people to Christ in such a public forum. I wasn't good at any of that. I was a very shy child, and if there were more than three strangers in a room, I would run away screaming. I did that a lot. I acted this way well into my teens (maybe minus the screaming), and I'm not proud of it, but it was just who I was. Guess what? God didn't regret calling me and knew who I was when He did.

I was blessed enough to know what my calling was at sixteen, but I ran from it. I was absolutely terrified by the prospect. You see, at that age I didn't understand that God calls the seemingly unqualified things of this world to demonstrate His power, as we see in 1 Corinthians 1:27:

> But God has chosen the foolish things of the world to put to shame the wise, and God has chosen the weak things of the world to put to shame the things which are mighty.

God equips the called; He rarely calls the equipped. Compare my situation to Jesus being born in circumstances we would certainly not choose for the King of Kings. This is the pattern of God's way, so that it is very evident the success comes from God, not man's abilities. Gideon was a young man whom God called to lead Israel in war against the evil Midianites. Gideon responded to the call:

> So he said to Him, "O my Lord, how can I save Israel? Indeed my clan is the weakest in Manasseh, and I am the least in my father's house." (Judges 6:15)

Gideon was terrified and was actually hiding in a winepress, which is a shallow hole in the ground, when the angel spoke to him. He did not want to fight with his brothers in the war, but God said to Gideon:

> And the Lord said to him, "Surely I will be with you, and you shall defeat the Midianites as one man." (Judges 6:16)

Wow. Can you see God views us in our full potential and not in our circumstances? Gideon obeyed and went on to lead Israel to a great victory, without any of the Israelites having to even unsheathe a sword. Sadly, I did not obey as Gideon did. Looking back on that time, I can see that I was actually ready, if I had only stepped out in faith and obedience. I won't say I had a "Jonah experience," where I ran in the opposite direction of God's call in disobedience, but instead of answering the call, I busied myself with things not related to pastoral ministry that would bring me temporary joy. I justified my actions by saying, "God opened this door for me." He might have opened some of them, but I know now that my success was purely due to His grace, and the purpose of any success I had was to learn, grow, and be prepared for what He ultimately had planned all along. Even in this "side journey" from the call, God knew exactly what He was doing. He was using my "detour" to prepare me for a very specific purpose.

In these God-given (or God-allowed) business opportunities, I began to develop myself and gain confidence. Of course, before this all made sense to me, I didn't trust that God knew what He was doing. My wife and I worked hard to have enough money as well as a successful business and a good life. We owned a custom home on a hill with four bedrooms, four and one-half baths, and three stories that overlooked our entire city. We had two Mercedes parked in the driveway and a BMW motorcycle that mostly sat in the garage. I had amazing, beautiful things that I loved to show off to people. I told people how much God had blessed me, but if I was honest, deep down there was a huge emptiness because the calling on my life was constant, and I wasn't responding to God, while time slipped away.

Then I fell into the enemy's guilt trap. While I was more than happy to show off my business success, I was afraid to share the calling on my life because I felt like a hypocrite. If I told people what I was really created to do, how would they respond? Would they say, "Dustin, we know you. We know the sin in your life. How can you tell others about their sin or share the word of God when you live the way you do?" As time went on, the hypocrisy became worse: *What would my friends say? How could I tell them God has called me to something bigger in my life?*

Strangely enough, my deepest fear was sharing my calling with my wife. More than anyone else, she knows all my imper-fections. She knows my anger, my secrets, and my sin, but one day, after I was just too unsatisfied with everything else, I knew she was the first one I had to be honest with. It was a *very* scary moment, but at the age of twenty-four, I finally told Sara the truth about God's calling on my life. I was terrified and had no idea what her reaction would be, but I knew I had to tell her; I just couldn't go on ignoring the call.

You see, this is the thing. Romans 11:29 says, "For the gifts and the calling of God are irrevocable." The Holy Spirit will never let up on you because you were created for a specific purpose and He *knows* you can fulfill it. Ignoring the call doesn't make it any easier. So I asked Sara if I we could discuss something, and she (probably nervously) agreed; we sat down, and I began to pour out my heart. I explained that I knew I hadn't been the best husband or friend, but I was certain this was the direction God was leading me. And I made it very clear that I would do anything necessary to make this a reality. Sara did not respond in the way I'd feared; in fact, her reaction was quite the opposite. Being the "Proverbs 31" woman that she is, Sara was nothing but supportive and so excited for me. I cannot tell you what a blessing that was and yet another confirmation that God had given me exactly the right wife.

Sara could tell how serious I was, and she agreed to us simply listing our new home we'd just purchased and selling our extra cars. I rid myself of these material possessions because, for me personally, it was a necessary step in following God's call. I knew people in my community would look at me and ask how I could reach the lost when I lived such an "over the top" lifestyle, so I wanted to remove the stumbling block. It is true that God had blessed us and given us the opportunity to buy those things, but I knew that I couldn't reach those who were down on their luck when I was going home to a life of luxury. Why would they listen to me? How could they respect what I had to say? They couldn't relate. What faith did I have if I didn't rely on God to feed, clothe, or shelter me?

I gladly gave up my worldly treasures to answer God's call because as soon as I answered the call, I was fulfilled. I had entered the specific purpose God intended for my life, and I knew it. Now, I mentioned God's grace earlier, but I want to reiterate that concept here. God knew exactly whom He was calling and what He was doing when He called me. I was so afraid to speak in public or attend social gatherings that I chose to be alone, and I preferred my own company because it was "safe." How could God call someone like me to lead when I am afraid to speak in public and to strangers? Well, let me say again that I was definitely no surprise to God, and neither are you. God knows the challenges we will face from the day we're born. He doesn't measure us by these worldly standards, however; He measures us by our potential in Jesus Christ. This is why, in hindsight, I can clearly see God has allowed situations I could never have imagined to push me out of my comfort zone and prepare me "for such a time as this."

Since the inception of my professional life and all of the related experiences, hard work, and time accumulated doing that, God continued molding and crafting me into a vessel that was prepared to do His will. One thing I know for sure is that God's ways are not our ways, and He can accomplish His plan for your life despite our "detours." This should be very encouraging to you right now. I know it was to me when I realized this fact. In my case, there was a "background" of slow but steady commitment to God, an obedience in many situations, and a continual yearning to fulfill His calling. In time, God enabled me to no longer be afraid to engage people or to speak in public. In fact, I could address a crowd of thousands or share the hope I have in Jesus to a total stranger. This is nothing short of miraculous and, of course, is essential to effective pastoring.

So here's the point of this chapter: know without a doubt that you're called for a very specific purpose and know that it's never too late to fulfill your calling. Jesus was born in a lowly feeding trough, but God wasn't surprised by the circumstances (in fact, He planned it that way). God is not surprised that you are where you are right now; He can and will help you still fulfill your calling. The thing is, you have to take the step today; even if it's taking one small step, take that step.

May I ask: Do you know what God is calling you to do? His plan is completely different for everyone, but if you spend some time listening to Him, God will reveal the first step of your calling to you. It's the most exciting experience in the world when God reveals your calling because it is what all your gifts, talents, desires, and excitement revolve around. He won't call you to something you hate. If you're an engineer, He won't call you to creative writing—unless that's also part of your gift. If you're an actor, He won't call you to be an insurance actuary (unless...yep, that is also part of your gift). You were created for a very specific purpose, so obviously your calling will rely on who God created you to be. But it still takes courage. You will have to step out of your comfort zone in some way; the question is, will you be willing to answer that call when it comes in? It will almost certainly move you out of your safe places, and sometimes that is scary.

God might call you to move to a different country, give up some of your creature comforts, quit a job, start a job, mend relationships, or do a myriad of other things. What matters is the bottom line: no matter our weaknesses, our fears, or our hang-ups, when God calls us, we need to follow Him because He will work out the rest. It's not for us to figure out every detail. Don't you think He has it taken care of? Your only job is to say, "Yes!" be obedient in what He has called you to, and then trust Him.

Maybe God has called you, but you haven't done anything about it. You *must* stop running. God promises good for those of us who love and obey His commandments, and that includes your calling. He promises hope and a future, and that is tied into your very specific purpose. The things we hold on to don't matter in eternity. I would much rather seek God's will wholeheartedly than halfheartedly work a job I wasn't called to do, in a home I don't need, wearing clothes I could've lived without, with an emptiness inside that only Jesus can fill.

Before I made the decision to completely follow God's call, it was as if I had been driving a speedboat. A top-of-the-line, always-gassed-up speedboat, ready to take me wherever I wanted to go. Once I made the decision to pursue God's call, it felt more like a sailboat. I now rely on God's Spirit to blow my sails wherever He wishes. And I am a thousand times more satisfied with my life now, relying on God to guide and direct me. Are you in the speedboat or the sailboat? Are you searching for things that God never intended for you to search for, and could that be the source of your emptiness? Have you been patient, quiet, and truly open to hear God's call? Every Christian will have a specific calling, but the one call that ties them all together is to go out and preach the good news to all creation. You can always start there. Get in your sailboat, cast out your net, and wait. God will fill it until it overflows. He is waiting for you; are you ready?

17

An American Dream?

Do you remember when I promised you this book would have some ideas that challenge your comfort zone? Well, this is definitely going to be one of those chapters. I want to ask you: Have you ever woken up in the middle of the night, sweating and shaking, from a really scary nightmare? I have. I don't know if you've experienced this, but it's even worse when you can't remember the dream. This actually happens to me a lot for some reason. I'm not quite sure why; perhaps it's stress, an overactive imagination, or maybe both.

Alternately, have you ever had a magnificent dream from which you didn't want to wake? We have a dog. He's a very special dog (as his name reflects): Mr. Pablo Baggins. Pablo is a seven-pound Yorkie who was surnamed "Baggins" because I brought him home one evening in a fast food bag to surprise Sara. Pablo was supposed to be a teacup Yorkie, but he turned into more of a coffee mug. He's a rather crazy dog who is very possessive of his favorite bear, Amadeus, and sometimes when he dreams, it wakes me. It's interesting because most of the time, it's really tough to tell if Mr. Baggins is having a good dream or a nightmare. He'll be asleep on his back, moaning and whining and shaking, and I'll nudge him awake to reassure him he hasn't lost all his bones or isn't getting a bath (surely, this is what qualifies as a doggy nightmare). My only hope is I'm not waking him from a dream of mountains of dog treats and a glorious roll in some soupy mud.

Interestingly, whenever people ask me how work is going, I always respond with the catchphrase, "Oh, you know, just living the dream." I say it for a laugh, but I have to ask myself: *Is it true? Am I living THE dream? And what exactly is that?* I actually think about that a lot. And more importantly: *Was I called to live a dream?* It is commonly said that people from other countries come to American to pursue the "Great American Dream," but let's ask ourselves: What is that in the twenty-first century? James Truslow Adams tried to define this idea in 1931 when he wrote, "Life should be better and richer and fuller for everyone, with opportunity for each according to ability or achievement." He was saying these objectives should be achievable regardless of creed, color, or social caste. The American Dream is supposed to be the pursuit of hope, freedom, opportunity, and a better life, but let's be honest—I have worked very hard, as I am sure most of you have, but my life doesn't quite match up with this notion of "The American Dream."

"That's crazy!" you may say. "You are living it; you have experienced success, have some savings, a good marriage, you work for yourself..." Those things are true, and I'm extremely grateful for them, but there was a deep emptiness at one point, despite having all of these things. Why was that?

In the American Dream, you are supposedly able to be anything you desire and do anything you set your mind to by starting out with a dream of fortune, freedom, and greatness. In the fifties, the American Dream was to have opportunities for success and equality, be comfortable, have a steady job, own a home, and raise a family. Now that we have begun the twenty-first century, what is our modern American Dream? Tens of millions of American workers aren't even earning a livable wage, yet we're working more than ever. Most stores are open on weekends, and some are open twenty-four hours a day, but we're unhappier than ever.

One of the biggest industries in America is pharmaceuticals, prescribing uppers for when we're down and downers for when we can't get back down to sleep. (Did you know the United States and New Zealand are the only countries in the world that are allowed to commercially advertise drugs direct to consumers?) The credit card industry is a global leader, with most Americans enslaved in debt with an average of over $15,000 per person at the time of this writing. Our cars are often leased, our homes often rented, and we're usually working over sixty hours a week. Our youth follow unrealistic role models of professional athletes or musicians or reality TV stars, who make up less than 1 percent of those sacrificing wise decisions to aspire to those goals. We find ourselves with broken dreams and the ruins of what are most certainly delusions. I ask myself: What kind of dream is this?

A while back, one of my dreams was to win the lottery. I don't know why, but I got so caught up in playing the lottery that I played every single day for several weeks straight and was fully confident I would at least win my money back. Surely the odds are better when you play that much, right? (Wrong, actually. Sadly, the terrible odds are the same each time you play.) This is what my American Dream had become, and the larger the jackpot grew (it peaked at $297 million), the bigger my dream became. I mean, can you even comprehend that much money? I started to dream about how I'd spend it all. I'd even decided to take the yearly payout over the cash option (remember how much I hate taxes?) and did the math to calculate how much I could spend every year for the next fifty years. I figured if I died at seventy-five...well, I would have a whole lot of spending to do before then. First, I'd need a classic car, a designer home, and a passport full of stamps from exotic places around the world. And that would just take care of the first few months. The problem was that I had also been dreaming my wife wouldn't be mad at my decision to spend our money this way if she found out. Again, it was a delusion, because she did find out and needless to say, she was very, very angry. *Oops!*

Now sure, we all have personal dreams and a picture of how our lives should go. It may not be cars, homes, or clothes, but I'm sure you have a dream or at least a desire of how your life will look one day. A boss that isn't so mean? A raise? To pay off your student loans? Perhaps it's to find your soul mate? Growing up, like so many other young men, I was always hyperconscious about the car I drove. It had to be cool, fast, and have a great sound system, and I believed I needed a new one every year. Looking back, I can see I wasted so much money on that goal. Once I had attained that goal, I needed new clothes, and after that, I needed a large home. When Christmastime came around, I had to outdo everyone else with my creativity and the amount of money spent. On and on and on it went, never really being enough; my appetite for more was insatiable.

The interesting thing is that when I started shifting my focus toward Christ over the years, my dreams began to change significantly. The difference was that I made a decision to find my true calling and I finally was able to give my all to Christ, and it was at this point that my desires began to change. I didn't have to manufacture anything nor feel like I should be doing a better job. I simply allowed the Holy Spirit to modify my focus and calling in Jesus Christ, and the material longings began to dwindle away.

Now, don't get me wrong. What changes is that you begin to gain a more a practical view of material things; for example, I am very happy with my Volkswagen. I need a reliable car; it isn't lavish, but it has some nice features like power windows and locks that keep me from being stressed out. I am also elated when I find the sales racks at the shops in the mall, and after wasting tons of money on a home that I did not need, I started renting a modest apartment, saving thousands of dollars each month. These are things I need, and I believe with all of my heart God is happy to give them to me. The difference is that these things are a means to an end—pursuing my calling. The best news from this scenario is that a practical focus on finances frees my heart to focus on God and on serving Him and following His will.

When you start focusing on God and His heart and desires, your thoughts will also change. What will that kind of vision look like? For starters, you won't worry about keeping up with the Joneses or impressing your friends. You'll know in your heart that your worth is already established in Christ, and nothing can ever change that. As you grow and begin your service, you'll see how truly prestigious it is serving Almighty God. When you are focused on Christ, your vision and heart will change naturally. Your primary dream will be to reach lost souls for Christ, even though many of us have gifts that may be helping in the local church. It all boils down to the same thing: you'll want to share the love of Christ and the hope you have in Him. You'll want every person on this planet to know there is more to this life than what they are living right now. Most people have no idea...and that's truly a crying shame.

Winning souls is really the only dream I want to pursue. And, friend, believe me, Christ has an amazing dream for you too, one that will completely fulfill you. You just need to refocus your thoughts. You do that by submitting, in obedience, to God's calling, whatever it is (the Holy Spirit will tell you). But you need to start seeking Him to find it. In the process, your life will no longer be about the accumulation of possessions or wealth or the perfect guy or girl. Instead, it will be dedicated to a purpose with eternal rewards: following Christ.

I'd much rather chase after God's dream and vision for my life than try to fill myself with the shallow pleasures the world advertises to make itself rich and will never truly satisfy me. Friend, we cannot fathom what God has in store for us, and we will only realize just how huge God's plans are for us when we take that first step and truly start seeking His calling in prayer and study of the Word. He knows what will ultimately fulfill us, and as I've said in the previous chapter, you have very specific gifts and tendencies for a reason. When you refocus your mind through a continuous relationship with the Lord, He'll automatically form a new dream in which you chase after His heart and His heart alone. And that's a truly mind-blowing dream. In fact, it's the only dream that matters in this lifetime because His dream for your life is *tailor-made* for you.

Recently, I was running on the treadmill and thinking it is probably one of the only times in my day that I wish could fly by. I cannot wait for that hour to be completed, but in practically every other area of my life, I pray time will slow down. Some people may wish their time at the DMV would go faster or that those eight grueling hours at a dead-end job would speed up so they can go home and relax on the couch.

Wishing time away is the fastest way to waste your life and *the surest sign you are not fulfilling your calling.*

By the time you are thirty years old, you have lived nearly eleven thousand days. How many of those days were lived on purpose? How many friends have you invited to church? How many people heard about the gospel from you? I was in the exact same boat, so these questions are not meant to shame you but rather to put things in perspective. For many years, I didn't live my life with purpose. Many of my readers are older than thirty, and I am sure you have accomplished much, but maybe you are just starting your faith journey. Maybe you have been too afraid to share your relationship with Jesus with others. My goal is to simply show you the reality of the situation and encourage you to get started. Because it's the most amazing journey you can ever take; it's what you were created to do.

By that age, you have most likely completed high school or received your GED and maybe attended college. Perhaps you went straight into the workforce with a full-time job, or preferred to pursue graduate school. I am so impressed with my wife because she received her master's degree by the age of twenty. That is such a phenomenal accomplishment, and I am so very proud of her, but at the end of the day (and she'll agree with this), does it matter as much as someone coming to know the Lord? I'm not at all saying a graduate degree is not important; in fact, I believe it can be very useful in areas of ministry. However, if your calling in Christ *has not* been your focus so far, think about each individual day, the opportunities that have passed you by, and the people that could've received hope and salvation. How many people have you met in those thousands of days that needed to know about God?

Fast forward fifteen years and imagine you are forty; by that time, you will have lived close to fifteen thousand days. If you live to be seventy years old, you have lived more than twenty-five thousand days. Each day is a gift, and the most wasteful thing we can do is forget to treat it as such. I certainly don't want my tombstone to read, "Had good intentions but never made a change." I want to change lives; I want to share the hope I have in Jesus and tell people about their purpose. How selfish is it to not share this unfathomable and unearned gift with others? Remember where the unsaved are destined for, whether they know it or not.

Instead, some of us run on a treadmill for miles but go nowhere. We do that in life, pursuing that which really doesn't matter. We miss opportunities God puts in front of us because we are too focused on ourselves. I am not pointing any fingers; I am guilty of this too! I am praying for constant change and purposing in my heart to follow God. I wait in anxious anticipation of what God can do with a willing heart. It is so easy to get caught up in our daily to-do lists and focus on things that will make us happy, but if we only seek God with our entire hearts, He will take care of all those things.

When I meet the Lord in heaven, I want Him to say, "Dustin, well done, My good and faithful servant," not "Dustin! What did you do you with all of your talents, son?" I want to invite thousands of people to church and share the good news about Jesus with them, not because I have to or because it's my Christian duty, but because there are lost people walking around who deserve to know the hope that is in Jesus Christ.

Maybe you wished away many of those days. We all do it. When we are children, we want to be sixteen and have the freedom to drive. Then, we can't wait to turn eighteen, finish high school slavery (as it seems), and become adults. Then we can't wait to finish college so we can land that elusive "dream job" in search of...the American Dream. The funny thing is, any person older than thirty will tell you that high school and college (if he or she attended) were some of the best years of his or her life. Do you see how we're wasting away our lives, hoping and dreaming for the next milestone? If we simply focus on God's calling, every day will have a purpose; every day will be full of growth and a hope-filled adventure.

So in this chapter, I invite you to do the math: How often are you living for yourself, and how often are you living for God? I want to live my life with purpose, don't you? How sad would it be to wish away your days or endlessly hope for the next chapter in your life to start, only to realize one day you've been chasing an empty illusion? The truth is that we have only really been given today; there is simply no promise for tomorrow on this earth. For that reason, I refuse to sit on the couch all day, thinking about the great and amazing changes I will make *tomorrow* or *could have* made yesterday but never started. I promise you the only way to truly live the Great Adventure is to step into God's calling for your life. I personally want to go wherever God tells me to go, and I am willing to step out of my comfort zone. I want to meet new people who need to know the Lord and do my utmost to save their eternal souls from the unthinkable! That is the reality of our mission.

Friend, the Heavenly Dream for your life is unfathomable! God says His ways are not our ways and His thoughts are not our thoughts. He has plans for you that are so tremendous He can't share the full picture with you right now because you're simply not ready! It would blow your mind. Please, do not read this book and just go back to sitting on the couch. Do anything you can, even if you start small. If you aren't praying or reading the Bible each day, start praying for five minutes a day and reading one scripture. Next week, pray for ten minutes a day and read two scriptures a day. Maybe just pass this book along to a friend or, better yet, start applying these principles in your own life. God will lead you.

Just as babies learn to crawl before they can walk, you can start your journey with small changes. With time and faith, they will *snowball* into much bigger ones. I encourage you to no longer live in fear. I mean, honestly, what would really happen if you invited a friend or family member to lunch and very lovingly told them about what God is doing in your life? There is nothing easier to share nor more powerful than your personal testimony. It's a direct witness and proof of what God is doing! Sharing this won't be nearly as disastrous as you imagine. In fact, what if it is just the thing he or she needs to start asking questions about Jesus? What if you end up winning someone into the kingdom and changing your loved one's eternal destiny? So I challenge you to ask yourself, "Am I going to continue doing the same unfulfilling things, day in and day out, believing the 'someday' delusion? Or am I ready to take a leap of faith, trusting that God only wants good for those He loves?"

Chase after Christ. Accept your calling. I'm confident you won't waste your life, and I guarantee you won't be disappointed.

18

House Hunters versus Kingdom Hunters

Sara and I watch a lot of HGTV, and one show we especially enjoy is *House Hunters*. For us, it's usually very satisfying watching people deciding between various choices, choosing their new homes, and starting new lives while being truly happy about it. Sometimes, however, I feel frustrated when people are so picky that you quickly realize they will never be content with any option. You can tell right from the start of the episode that these people will never find what they are looking for (perfect solutions rarely exist). In fact, if I hear them say they use a "hundred-point scale" to find a home, I immediately tune out or change the channel.

This scale supposedly helps them prioritize everything they "need" in a home; one of them almost always being a gargantuan walk-in closet. In so many episodes, the wife will make the exact same joke; she'll look in the master closet and say, "Well, this closet is big enough for me, but where will you put all your things, honey? Ha-ha!" The realtor forces a stale laugh because he or she heard that joke *ad nauseam*, but the bottom line is that they all make the same joke out of a place of discontent.

The "must have" often won't even consider a house without granite countertops, a wine fridge, and vaulted ceilings, and sometimes the *House Hunters* will declare a home simply unlivable if the cabinets are stained the wrong shade. I'm not trying to sound holier than thou, but you should watch an episode like that after a day spent with the Lord. One has to wonder: *Do they truly <u>need</u> Napa Merlot Rosé cabinet stain with blue granite countertops and a brushed-steel wine fridge? Really?* Maybe there isn't much about the show I like, after all. It actually stresses me out! These people are searching for a perfect home that doesn't exist, but I guess that makes for addictive television.

Of course, they say we dislike in others what we dislike in ourselves. If I'm honest, I must admit I am guilty of the same avarice. We moved to California four years ago and since then, we have moved *five* times. At first, an apartment wasn't good enough, so I needed to rent a lovely, spacious home. Next, I needed to own a home in order to increase my social standing, but it couldn't be just any old home; I went *House Hunters* crazy. I *needed* a home that would impress and be the cause of social envy. My greed (er...I mean, need) didn't end there; I obviously *needed* flashy cars to go with the ostentatious house.

At the time, I believed these possessions were filling a legitimate need in my life, yet for some reason, I still I felt empty. I won't lie; the consumerism was initially satisfying, but it soon ebbed…often quickly and sometimes even with no small amount of buyer's remorse. When that happened, I tried to refill the void by throwing lavish parties and entertaining high-status guests, even letting people borrow my slick cars to show how generous I was. I would claim, "God blessed me so I could bless others," and although there was some truth in that statement, God knew the full motivation of my heart. I'm not saying having nice stuff is wrong; owning a big house or a great car does not make you a bad person. I can admit I love granite countertops and Mercedes sedans. The problem comes in when the stuff *owns you*.

For the first four years of my marriage, my wife and I probably ate at home *fifty* times. Think about that…four years multiplied by 365 days a year equals 1,460 days. Sara is a terrific cook, but I was bored (apathetic), had good income, and was looking for something to fill the void in my life. We regularly argued over our eating habits; Sara begged me to eat at home, correctly stating it's healthier, saves money, and is something she just enjoys. But I wouldn't listen; I wanted to be out in the community, seeing how other people lived. I didn't want to sit in my huge, boring home! I wanted to go out and drop more cash in restaurants of all kinds.

Please hear me. If God has blessed you with material possessions, He wants you to enjoy the fruits of your labor and the gifts He has given you, but the difference is the attitude of your heart—your *focus*. In time, I was thankful to have learned I am personally called to live differently because at that point, the stuff honestly *had me*. It was a stumbling block, and it was choking out the Word in my heart. Now, I can no longer bring myself to live lavishly and above our means when I directly know people who are barely making ends meet, with no money left at the end of the month.

I'll never forget an experience while on a mission trip to Guatemala when I was eighteen. Each day, we served the poor community by building prefabricated houses for the homeless. However, each night, we dined like comparative kings. I'm talking buffets, a steak dinner, and very generous homemade meals. We were never hungry, even for a moment, and that was when I began feel uneasy; my considerable advantages in life slowly (and painfully) dawned on me.

One day, we drove to a small village to build a home for a woman named Margarita. Margarita's "home" to be wasn't much more than four brick walls with a single window. It was literally just one room; there was no kitchen and no separate sleeping quarters, and in place of a bathroom, there was only a bucket behind a skimpy curtain in the corner. Outside, an assortment of animals ran through the neighborhood while dirty children played in the sand "roads" beside a stream of sewage running right next to the home.

I was part of the bricklaying team. It was my first time ever doing anything like that and by this point, I even felt ashamed of my lack of skills. Despite the meager accommodations and obvious inexperience of the team, however, Margarita could not stop smiling. She had so little and was somehow getting by on almost nothing; she was entirely grateful we were building this lavish, one-room home for her. She treated us like knights in shining armor.

Margarita didn't get to choose the color of the walls or the type of flooring (packed dirt). She didn't have a choice of quartz or granite countertops or oak or walnut furniture; she was just overwhelmingly happy that she would have a roof over her head. It rocked my world and made no sense to me. I knew soon after I met Margarita that we could all learn a lesson from this sweet woman. Could I honestly say I'd be happy with what she was given? Would I be grateful to have a cold, brick, one-room home? Or would I demand more?

Again, don't get me wrong. God wants good things for our lives, and He wants to take care of us. As I've mentioned before, if you live in America or a Western democracy, you likely have a very easy life, comparatively. In fact, the majority of Americans are considered wealthy when compared to most of the world. Yet, when I see how little others live on and yet how their lives are still so rich, I realize something drastically needs to change in my heart. I would get by just fine without a fancy home, a sweet ride, and nightly meals out. It just doesn't make sense to live so extravagantly when you know others go to bed hungry, sleep in a box, and have very little hope for a better future. It just doesn't feel right to call myself a Christian while taking so much for myself and giving nothing to those in need. At the end of the day, it comes down to love.

> But whoever has this world's goods, and sees his brother in need, and shuts up his heart from him, how does the love of God abide in him? (1 John 3:17)

When we moved to California to open the restaurant, my goal was *never* to move back to Florida! I loved California. However, as is so typical of God, He had other plans—better plans. All of a sudden, I felt God was calling me back there, but I had to ask myself if that was true. While I loved California, had the Lord called me back to Florida, or was I simply more comfortable where things felt familiar? Was it easier to live there because the cost of living is so much lower and we have family there?

Recently, an opportunity to move back to Orlando popped up out of the clear blue, and immediately we saw it as an answer to prayer and a sign God was moving us back home. We knew we would be able to buy a home on some land without paying an arm and a leg. We also have friends in Florida we have missed, and we could go out to eat more frequently because everything is cheaper. A far more convenient life called to us from Orlando, yet as we moved forward with the transition, I felt deep in my heart that God was not in it.

Despite that check in my spirit, I spent a month scheduling interview after interview, making countless phone calls, and writing e-mails to make the move a reality. I convinced myself it could be where God wanted us since a clear door had opened. On the surface, it looked like a great opportunity that could have afforded us two franchise locations in the future, but deep down, I felt uneasy. Something (Someone?) tugged at my heart, and I just knew it wasn't the right step for us; we could have made it work. But was it what God ultimately wanted for us? No, it wasn't. Thankfully (as tough a pill as it was to swallow), God led us to let go of it.

The point is that we so often talk ourselves into situations that we think are best for us, and we end up accumulating things we think we need; all the while, God may have different plans. I knew from the beginning God wasn't present in my relocation opportunity, but I persisted longer than I should have and spent much (wasted) time and energy on that pursuit. I must be honest; while I might have been more comfortable in Orlando for while, there is a reason God called me to California, and I feel the joy of walking in His purpose while I'm here. Maybe one day, I'll be back in Florida with my family, but for now, God wants me in California, and I want to pursue Him and find out what that reason is.

I want to clarify again that God wants you to have a good life; He wants you to make money, but we must understand that money is also a means to and end. We need to understand the heart of the matter is that it's really not *our* money.

God gives it to us with a specific plan in mind for our lives; don't ever believe the money is yours. A good way to think of it is that we are merely stewards and that how we manage our resources will reflect our reward as well.

Now, when I talk about resources, I am talking about more than just your money. In a way, your money reflects your talents and life effort of the work you do, and ultimately, even if you are working a job outside of ministry, you can still devote that time to the Lord. This is the upside of understanding the Lord blesses you with even your job. In Matthew 25:14–30, Jesus told a parable of three different men, each of whom had been given a certain amount of talents—or money—by their master and were told to earn a return on the money. (Yes, the dual English meaning for talent being inherent abilities is very interesting.)

The first servant was given five talents. He invested them well and earned a 100 percent return (five more talents). The second servant was given two talents, and he too earned a 100 percent return (two more talents). The third servant was given just one talent, but he took his talent and buried it in the ground so it would be safe. I imagine he figured it was only one talent; if he lost it, he would lose everything, and he figured it wouldn't be a big deal if he just returned it to his master as is. But the man didn't understand the *cost of investment*.

The master returned and praised the servant who had ten talents, saying he was faithful with a little and as a result, he would make him ruler over much. He did the same with the second servant, but when it came to the third man, the master was furious. The servant said he knew the master was a hard man, and he didn't want to lose his investment. The master called the servant wicked and lazy, telling the servant he knew his master was a hard man, yet he still didn't do everything he could to get a return on his investment. He then gave the talent to the servant with ten talents, showing that God takes His investments in people *very* seriously. In the parable, the master threw the lazy servant into *outer darkness*. That should get our attention.

I think you can read between the lines. (Actually, the point is quite plain. I encourage you to read Matthew 25:14–30 for yourself.) I want to go back to the fact, however, of the interesting dual meaning of the word *talent*. Sure, it means money in the original Greek translation, but when you read that scripture passage, it actually says each servant was given an amount *according to his ability*. That means God knows what we're capable of. It also means you can underperform and it will greatly displease God.

My point here is that you may say, "I don't live comfortably, Dustin; I'm barely making ends meet. How can I sacrifice even more?" Well, you have unique talents, and here I mean the English word, meaning the inherent ability to pick up certain things quickly. You can use those skills for God, even when you don't have much or don't necessarily work directly in ministry. I've heard of so many stories where people volunteered in their spare time, doing something they love, and it turned into a job or opened a door of opportunity to make much more money or even a way to enter full-time ministry. What I'm saying is that if your heart is right and you put the kingdom first, God will reward you and give you more to do, so you can have more influence. This is very different from giving you more to squander; in fact, from the rest of the chapter, we know that although He loves us, it becomes very difficult for Him to bless us if we are hoarders seeking greed, instead of what we need to further the kingdom.

So I've decided that, ultimately, I want to give everything in my life back to Christ so it will be a testimony to how God has changed my life and can change the lives of others too. I want to build up my treasures in heaven, not earth. Can you ask yourself: Where are your treasures? Are they on earth, or are they being stored up for heaven? Are you walking through the doors that God has opened for you, or are you convincing yourself God wants the same things that you do? Have you even sought His will in that regard? More importantly, are you using your talents (money and skills) with a kingdom focus or selfish focus?

I've come to the place where, more than anything, I want to honor God in everything I do. I want to bring people closer to God, and I want you to walk closer to God. If you know the Holy Spirit has been convicting you about material things that are in your way, maybe it's time you think about seeing if someone less advantaged needs those things more. Once you are kingdom minded and, in your heart, give it all over to Jesus, I guarantee your life will be less stressful and more joyful. You can rest knowing you don't need to have every detail of your life planned out; instead, you will rely on the Holy Spirit.

That's the beauty of obedience; this isn't some test where God, in some form of twisted cruelty, wants to see if we will afflict ourselves to show our loyalty to Him. No! That is so far from His nature. God wants us to shift our focus to kingdom mindedness so He can give us what we need when our focus is lined up with His. When we rest in that knowledge, we don't have to stress or worry anymore, we don't have to keep up with the Joneses, and we don't have to feel alone or afraid because it's now God's problem. This attitude, my friends, is one of the most critical yet overlooked steps in finding your calling, but when you begin to shift your focus to serving the kingdom, I promise you will have everything you need *and* the peace and joy that comes along with it.

One of the keys, however, is trusting in God's timing. Once you have a kingdom focus, when you learn to understand God's timing, you are actually beginning to walk in your calling. But more on that in the next chapter…

19

In His Timing

In this chapter, I'm going to talk about another one of the most critical lessons I've learned in discovering my calling. It's a simple concept, but that doesn't mean it's easy to integrate into your life. In fact, if every Christian could master this one habit, I believe we'd complete the work of Christ on this planet in a few short years. To truly begin walking in God's calling for your life, you will need to trust His timing.

If you've ever sat through a planning meeting, I'm sure you'll agree they are mind-numbingly boring and should be avoided at all costs. Wouldn't it be amazing, though, to attend one of God's planning meetings, especially if it was about your life? Well, it's nice to dream but unfortunately, we have to accept the fact that we can't always see what God is up to; even though we'd all love to be part of His planning meetings, they just aren't something we are privy to.

Planning is something we all do naturally, especially if you work in a position of leadership. Any leader knows he or she has to set goals for the future and show progress toward those goals. Planning for the future is imperative if you want to achieve any goals at all: things like graduate school, running a successful business, or even saving for a new car. I'll tell you now, however, it's impossible to plan our entire lives.

We can make plans for our financial future or where we aim to be in five, ten, even twenty years, but I'm sure God often sits back and chuckles when He hears our inane aspirations. The Lord hears what we talk about, dream about, and stress about, but consider that He has His own specific will for our lives and already knows the outcome of each situation. We spend so much time on planning. And don't get me wrong, planning is important—it gets us from point A to point B—but we need to remember that we should always consult God before we make any plans and above all, we must allow those plans to change as God wills. In fact, the Apostle James laid this out very clearly:

> Come now, you who say, "Today or tomorrow we will go to such and such a city, spend a year there, buy and sell, and make a profit"; whereas you do not know what *will happen* tomorrow. For what *is* your life? It is even a vapor that appears for a little time and then vanishes away. Instead you *ought* to say, "If the Lord wills, we shall live and do this or that." (James 4:13–15)

A few years ago, Sara and I began talking about starting a family; she didn't have to ask me twice. As I'm sure you've realized, I absolutely adore my wife and know she's the most beautiful woman I've ever seen, so naturally having children with her is something I'll sign up for immediately. I'll admit, though, at first I was pretty anxious when I thought about being a father, but I knew this would make Sara happy. It was not until we began trying to conceive that I realized it was all way more than I had bargained for. To add fuel to this fire, we believed having a baby would fix some of the problems in our marriage by forcing us to put down roots and finally establish a stable life.

We started trying in March 2012 and were elated when Sara was pregnant by May 2012. Sara scheduled a doctor's appointment and started telling everyone the exciting news. We were overjoyed to go to our first doctor's appointment together, but the mood was dampened when the doctor couldn't locate the 'fetal pole' or a heartbeat. He quickly allayed our fears, saying it was likely because the pregnancy wasn't far enough along, so we scheduled a follow-up appointment for a couple of weeks later.

At the second appointment, our worst fears were confirmed; there was no heartbeat, and we had lost the baby. The worst part was that Sara didn't have a natural miscarriage and had to have surgery to remove the fetus, which made the whole experience profoundly traumatic. This was the first time we'd tried to start a family, so we were shocked and reeling at the outcome. Those who have experienced a miscarriage know how devastating it is, but I was simply not prepared for how difficult it would be for my wife. As we shared our sad news with all who'd been celebrating with us just two weeks before, we discovered how common miscarriages are. This information did little to ease Sara's grief, of course; the bond between a mother and her baby, even right after conception, is supremely powerful. We were planning for an exciting new life, but we now felt like the rug was pulled out from under our feet.

Sometime after that, Sara and I went on a mission trip to Paris. (Yeah, it was a tough sacrifice, but someone had to do it!) It was an amazing experience. We had the opportunity to witness to people in Europe and see God working in France in a very cool way. Now, I don't speak any French, and Sara only knows a few words, so we naturally had some trouble communicating. For our first assignment, I was to make balloon animals, and Sara would paint children's faces. This was supposed to attract people to our group, where fluent French speakers could share the gospel with the parents. I had never made a balloon animal in my life before, but I quickly became proficient at making swords. Sara didn't have much in the way of face-painting skills either, so when the kids would ask her to be painted as a princess or Spider-Man, most of them walked away painted like a cat. Likewise, when they asked me for a hat, a boat, or a dog, they got a sword. Oh well. *C'est la vie*, as they say.

Before we started the actual missions part of the trip, however, we underwent some training. Our group was composed of about twenty people, many of whom had never shared their testimonies before. I had some experience, so I was sure I knew what the trainers were looking for. When the training began, the teacher asked us to form a circle and said he was going to call a couple of us up to share our testimonies in three minutes or less. (He actually had a stopwatch to keep track!) Well, he looked right at me and said, "You go first." *Okay*, I thought to myself. I wasn't nervous. *Three minutes? No problem, I can do it in two and a half!* I proceeded to give the most effective and moving version of my testimony in under three minutes flat, and when I was done, I looked expectantly at our group leader, confident he would dub me poster boy for all future testimony sharing. He ripped me to pieces. I mean, this guy really didn't take it easy on me and pointed out every little thing I did wrong. After a sound lambasting of about two minutes, it seemed as if he just wanted to make an example of me. When the soul crushing was over, I rejoined the circle and kept my mouth shut for the rest of the class.

Next, the guy called on my wife. I realized I had never asked her about her testimony before; I assumed she didn't really have one because she had grown up in a Christian home and attended church all her life. Her dad is a pastor, and she was a good kid, an agreeable teenager, and an upstanding adult, so I couldn't imagine what kind of testimony she could possibly share. After all, I didn't really know of any real pain she'd experienced.

What she shared blew my mind.

In Sara's three minutes, she talked about the loss of our baby. She explained how ecstatic she was when she fell pregnant and how utterly crushed she felt when she lost the child. She confessed how bitter and angry she became when she had the D and C (the surgery to remove the fetus). She said she didn't know whom to blame; sometimes she blamed herself, and sometimes she blamed God. Sara explained she just couldn't get over our thwarted plan to start a family; she couldn't understand *why* she'd had a miscarriage. Why did God allow our baby to die? Why did He allow us to conceive in the first place? In less than three minutes, years of pain, shame, and frustration were revealed in Sara's heart, but there was also a deep wisdom that had been produced from her experience.

It is in moments like that we can't always see God's plan for our lives. Yes, it's really difficult to see the future He holds for us, in the middle of dark times. It is during these times it's also very hard to see that the plans that last are His alone and rarely ours. We may try to make our own plans but ultimately, God commands and allows all things to take place in His perfect timing. If I think back to when Sara and I started talking about having a family, I can't even remember asking God for His input. I feel disappointed in myself that we never prayed about it.

When we started trying in 2012, my heart was not in it, but now we are both in agreement and ready to be parents.

Who knows what could have happened to our family if we had a child and I wasn't ready? Did God take our baby away? Of course not. The Bible says the *devil* comes to steal, kill, and destroy. But it happened nonetheless. What is interesting, though, is after seeking God about the decision to start a family, I felt God change my heart. Now that we are in a season of trying again, we have prayed and prayed and prayed about it, and we anxiously anticipate the future as parents.

Now I want to balance this message a little. All that being said, if God puts a desire or a longing in your heart, do not ignore it. Do not ponder it or mull it over without praying about it! Don't just talk to God about it once. Go to the Word and either find scriptures that promise what you are considering or learn more about what the Word says. If the Word doesn't agree with what you're wanting, give it up. If you can find anywhere in scripture where God promises the same thing for you, pray about it. Pray consistently and pray often. Pray with *expectant faith*.

Sara and I did this and as a result, we know the Bible says children a gift and a blessing from the Lord, so we are praying for our children that is yet to be born and she does that job with excellence already. If I didn't already let you in on the news, we had a beautiful baby girl in 2015! And another baby is on the way for 2016! God is faithful, and He is the giver of all good things. And for me, I can't wait to watch our kids grow up, help them with their homework, and most of all, teach them the Lord's ways.

When Sara was pregnant that time, our marriage was not in the best place. In fact, we had many challenges. We were carrying a huge mortgage payment and three car payments, had several people living with us, were running a new business, and as I mentioned, were living a lifestyle beyond what was necessary. We were about to add all the expenses and pressure that come with having a baby on to all that, so we felt stressed, to say the least. How would a baby have fixed any of our problems? It wouldn't have. As many know, a baby would more than likely have *amplified* our problems. Babies do bring stress and changes, but they are also a blessing from God. It definitely helps to seek God's timing, however, when starting a family.

Looking back on the miscarriage with fresh eyes, I understand why God didn't necessarily allow everything to go as we had planned. It actually blows my mind. When you pray for something and it doesn't happen, God is still God and has everything under control. Maybe you were passed over for a promotion, maybe you weren't accepted into your dream college, or maybe something happened that makes you believe your world is falling apart; God is still on the throne.

We may never know the reasons for everything that happens on earth, but I'm sure the Lord will explain it all to us in heaven if He wishes. Until then, *we simply have to trust Him*. I promise you events in your life have or have not taken place because He has a bigger plan. Perhaps you haven't learned a lesson you needed to learn, or maybe you would have been hurt or hurt someone else. We can't see the future, and we aren't supposed to. Have you heard the saying, "I don't know what the future holds, but I know who holds my future?" It may sound cliché, but it certainly is true.

Here's a secret: for you to truly take that next step in your calling, God needs to be able to trust you. Do you know how you reach the point where God trusts you? Yep! You learn to trust *Him*. The way we learn to trust Him is to daily draw nearer to Jesus, Who has promised hope and good things for us. As I said, it's simple, but it takes commitment. If you want to know your future and get a clear direction for your life, just draw near to God. He will guide you and give you peace that surpasses all understanding.

Now here's another perspective. When Sara fell pregnant, my brother was living with us. He was in a relationship with someone and believed there could be a future for them down the road. My brother had said outright he didn't want to live with us if we were going to have a baby. I could understand this, as babies cry a lot, and basically the entire household revolves around the little munchkin. To my brother's credit, he also wanted to give us the space to be a new family.

He told us several times that if Sara fell pregnant, he would move out, and I knew if we had a baby, it might put pressure on him to potentially rush into marriage with his girlfriend. What I also knew was that she was not the girl God wanted for him. This particular girl was filling a void for his comfort and conversation at the time, but I knew, and I think my brother knew deep down, that she was not "the one." When Sara fell pregnant, to my chagrin, they started talking about marriage, just as I predicted.

Another interesting perspective is that the miscarriage triggered a chain of events that brought my dad to Christianity. If we'd had a baby, my mom definitely wouldn't have left my dad and moved to California; therefore, my dad might never have been forced to reevaluate his life, hit his breaking point, subsequently find the Lord in a personal way. I can't say for sure that my brother would've married that girl or that my dad wouldn't have become a Christian, but I can say with confidence that God had a plan in mind all along. He knew what our future held, and true to His Word, He turned a terrible situation that the enemy meant for disaster into one that resulted in our family's ultimate good. Hindsight, as we know, is always twenty-twenty.

One question still remains, though: Why did God allow Sara to fall pregnant in the first place? Well, my personal opinion is that God allowed it because for one, we really wanted it, and maybe He allowed it to prepare us. We weren't ready financially, we weren't ready as a couple, and we weren't ready in our faith. Of course, you won't always be prepared for what

God has in store for your life, but He knows when something may be overwhelming for you. As we began to get our lives in order, the desire to have a family became stronger and stronger for us, and I believe we are now ready. We have sought the Lord, and I believe it is His will, and He will bless us with a child. We had to make some changes, though.

To find your calling, you'll also have to make some changes. Statistics show that only one in nine people will actually make the change they talk about. You can make a change today, but you must be willing to accept what God has in store: whatever highs, lows, excitements, or disappointments that may come your way, you must be ready and prepared to do whatever He wills. Whether God calls you to do something you never imagined you could do or calls you to stand up and give your testimony, just know He has it under control. He will never call you to do something you can't do. And remember, whatever He calls you to will *always* be the best thing for your life.

Getting started is easy; all you need to do is trust and pray. Maybe God did not allow us to have a baby in 2012 so that we could be blessed exponentially in different ways in the interim, yet it is still His vision and His plan in our lives that keep us moving forward. We are so blessed with the lives we have been given: our families, friends, jobs, and opportunities. Sara and I praise God each day for the blessings in our lives and continue to pray for the desires that are in our hearts.

So remember, as you draw nearer to God, remember He will reveal His will to you, but it will always happen in His time, not yours. Until then, be ready, because He is working on great things for you.

20

Trying to Out-Give God

Why do we have to reach our breaking point before we get on our knees and surrender to God? Why can't we just trust Him and, in obedience, know He will provide for our daily needs? I believe one of the biggest issues, at least with Western Christians, is that we so often worry we won't have enough to provide for our families. We fret about the car breaking down, worry we'll get sick, or worse, that we won't be able to keep up with the Joneses. Instead of focusing on "enough" to fulfill the call of God on our lives, we try to hoard resources for a "rainy day." This, sadly, turns into a materialistic focus, and it will handicap the call of God faster than just about anything else.

The truth is that focusing on provision is not a monetary or material crisis; it is a crisis of faith. If you are a follower of Jesus Christ, God has promised He will never leave you nor forsake you (Deuteronomy 31:6), nor will your children ever beg for bread (Psalm 37:5). He has your life in His control.

If you can accept this fact, you won't worry about anything! Matthew 6:25–27 says,

> "Therefore I tell you, do not worry about your life, what you will eat or drink; or about your body, what you will wear. Is not life more than food, and the body more than clothes? Look at the birds of the air; they do not sow or reap or store away in barns, and yet your heavenly Father feeds them. Are you not much more valuable than they? Can any one of you by worrying add a single hour to your life?" (Matthew 6:25–27) (NIV)

If you are devoted to finding and following the will of God for your life, the freeing truth is that there is no reason to worry about anything. What is the overarching will of God? He simply asks that we trust and obey Him. You'll have to figure it out on a day-to-day basis, but if you're serious about it, you'll hear His voice. You'll know what to do. When you do that, I promise you will be amazed by the doors that are opened and opportunities that are presented to you.

Sometimes, we forget God is so much smarter than we are. He knows your life; He knows what's going on and how you are struggling. He knows what you can handle and what is too much for you. But as you grow in faith, God will give you more. He may not always give you financial blessings, because He doesn't want you to become dependent or focused on money, but He will shower you with peace, security, consistency, and love.

There are not many instances in the Bible where God tells His people to test Him. In the book of Malachi, however, He says,

> "Bring all the tithes into the storehouse, that there may be food in My house, and try Me now in this," says the Lord of hosts, "If I will not open for you the windows of heaven and pour out for you such blessing That there will not be room enough to receive it." (Malachi 3:10)

That's a very powerful scripture that basically says God wants to outgive us. That may sound like just a nice sentiment, but it may not seem very realistic, right? Why would the God who rules over the universe want to give us things? It's hard to believe that if I give to Him, He will give back to me in *overflowing* amounts. But He promises to outgive us.

Have you ever really tried to outgive someone? My wife constantly accuses me of attempting to outgive her so I look like the better spouse. She really shouldn't feel this way because it's simply not true. Giving gifts is one of the primary ways I show my love; it's one of my love languages. But God is the biggest "outgiver" of all! He is constantly outgiving us, usually when we don't even realize it. No matter what we do, give, bring, or say, God will always meet and exceed what we do. That is just His nature because He is a loving parent. That realization also woke me up because I acknowledge now that there have been many times that I haven't given to God at all.

When Sara and I were called into ministry, we knew there were several things holding us back and distracting us from wholeheartedly serving God. We sold many of our material possessions, not out of obligation but out of the desire to be closer to God. One of the biggest obstacles was our home. As I've mentioned, we had a beautiful house that we truly loved. We enjoyed entertaining friends and sharing our home with others, but our mortgage was very high, and we knew it only made sense as godly stewards to downsize.

Thanks to a weak market, the house didn't move for almost a year. We finally sold it for the same price we had purchased it, but lost about $35,000 in commission. That was a very hard pill to swallow because some foolish decisions we'd made with our financial portfolio were catching up with us at the same time. We were young and made some poor financial choices, and it was time to pay the piper.

One of the worst decisions we made (or rather, did not make) was neglecting to set aside money at the end of the year to pay our taxes. Our income had increased, so we were suddenly told we were in a higher tax bracket, which would not have been an issue had we planned ahead, but it quickly became a very difficult year. It was our first year of marriage, we had just opened our business, and suddenly we had to take out a large loan just to pay our taxes. We misused the re-sources God gave us on nonsensical materialism, and we had nothing to show for it. We knew we really didn't *need* any of the things that we had lavishly spent money on.

The sale of our home felt like a weight lifted off us, but insecurity is an insidious trick of the enemy. Instead of continuing to trust God and trying to make amends for the frivolous spending we'd done, we made another mistake regarding our tithes. The tithe in the Old Testament is a tenth of your income set aside to give to the Lord. He had given us everything we had, asking only for 10 percent in return. We had lost money on our home and were now struggling to repay the loan we'd taken out for taxes, so we chose to stop tithing in favor of having some money in the bank.

I say "we," but as the spiritual leader of my home, I knew I was ultimately responsible for making the wrong decision. Seeing myself as the provider, however, I became pretty scared. Sara wanted to continue giving our tithe each month, but I made the final call and decided we just couldn't afford it. I was terrified I wouldn't earn enough money to cover our rent, bills, car payments, and food. I was focused on my own strength, which always causes you to operate solely in fear. We were trying to build up our financial cushion and pay off our loan, but Sara still wrote a tithe check each month. I'd have her file these checks away in her wallet, and soon the tithe checks and the guilt were piling up.

I don't know about you, but I find when we are budgeting every penny, it is way harder to give. That money could go to pay off debt or fix the car and remove some stress from our lives, but instead, we are explicitly called by God to tithe, regardless of the situation and regardless of whether or not it is convenient for us.

One day in church, God spoke directly to me. By that point, we were four or five months behind on our tithes, the checks still glaring at me from Sara's wallet. I was so convicted that I knew I had to change something. Feeling guilty and ashamed, we wrote a check for the total amount of all those checks combined and got ourselves "square" with God. We knew it would really hurt our bank account balance and might affect our ability to pay the bills, but the guilt was becoming too much for us. We know we had to be obedient. Skipping the tithes had added up quickly, but we knew that we had to give that money to the Lord like we should have been doing all along. We knew it was time to start honoring God again.

All we really wanted to do was repent and get ourselves right with God, but the next day, something amazing happened. A check arrived in the mail: a reimbursement for an overpayment of our health insurance from the prior year. The astonishing thing was it was the same amount of money we had tithed just the day before! I cannot tell you how good that felt. We had simply been obedient, and when we were, God didn't scold us or punish us for holding back that tithe. No, He rewarded us for our obedience! His love is so mind blowing, especially when you experience it firsthand like that. The point is that God wants to see your faith in action. We are so quick to forget He will provide for us, but He wants us to trust Him wholeheartedly with every aspect of our lives.

Another interesting point is the timing of God's provision in our experience. Do you remember when the pharaoh of Egypt changed his mind about letting the Israelites go and pursued them to the Red Sea? God waited until the very last minute to part the sea and make a way for His people to live, but He didn't fail them. The story doesn't end with, "And God allowed everyone to be killed because He just didn't come through for them that day." No! His people were saved because they had faith in Him, even in the most terrifying situation. He wanted to ensure the Israelites' faith was strong before He acted. God wants us to trust Him and desire Him. He wants us to hunger and thirst for Him, believing He can take care of us.

God wants to bless us, but if we are consistently disobedient, He may allow us to reach our breaking points. And believe me, if you become stubborn, He will allow whatever it takes for you to renounce your idols and get on your knees before Him. At that time in my life, God had blessed me abundantly and He had convicted me of materialism time and again, so eventually He had to allow me to fail. All of that success was taken from me. It makes sense; if you cannot be a good steward of what little God has given you, why would He entrust you with more? God wants great things for us. He desires for us to have rich, successful lives, and He knows He has a prosperous future for us, but He wants us to be spiritually mature as well. And when I say prosperous, I mean "having enough to fulfill His calling."

God needs to know we will make smart decisions. I made very poor financial choices that brought me to my breaking point before God. Through my mistakes, I learned that God will not share my devotion with idols (which we can even create from the gifts He gives us), but when I repent, He will always provide for me. He will part the Red Sea, and the glory will always belong to Him.

I am not a subscriber to the prosperity gospel, but I know God wants to bless us and give us full lives, just as you want the best for your children. You just might not be prepared for the plans and blessings He has in store for you right now—maybe because you haven't fully accepted His calling? So let's get ready. You cannot become a doctor, a professor, or coach in the NFL without training and working hard. You cannot be a surgeon just because you have a desire for it—you must start with the basics first and then grow and learn.

The same applies spiritually; we must prepare ourselves to receive the abundance God has for us. We should learn to be dependent on God. Most of us fought for our independence since we were teenagers, wanting to do everything on our own, but God did not design your relationship with Him to look like that. He wants to provide for you! He wants you to lean on Him and trust Him.

If we are truly honest with ourselves, we would admit we want to have more so we have to spend less time stressing about security. But what's your idea of "more"? Or what's your idea of security? For some, it is money or stability, while for others, it may be clout or friendships. That's our sinful nature looking to things of this world to satisfy a need only God can fill. If I may speak frankly, our goal is to reach a place where we don't need faith. I have done that plenty of times. I wanted to feel independent and self-assured so that I didn't have to trust or rely on God. But that isn't what a real relationship with God looks like.

Believe me, I have found far more peace by putting my faith in Him to provide for me than I ever did when I was do-ing it on my own. I urge you to take this very necessary step in finding and fulfilling God's calling. Give it a try. Get off the hamster wheel, because you aren't going to get anywhere. Take a leap of faith, trust in God, and see if He will not bless you more than you could have ever imagined when you align with His purpose. You are at the Red Sea right now. How will you cross it? All it takes is faith. Jump in and watch God work.

21

What If All Your Prayers Were Answered?

As a child, I remember that Christmas after Christmas, I would open my presents, only to be disappointed because I didn't get what I wanted. This happened year after year and did not change throughout my childhood. Only recently did I realize this was not my parents' fault; it was mine. I never received what I wanted because I never voiced my wishes to my parents. In fact, my parents asked me what I wanted for Christmas all year long but for some reason, I was too shy and never told them exactly what I wanted.

The funny thing is that I still do it with my wife. To add to the frustration, my birthday and Christmas are very close together, so it is difficult to separate the two with different presents. Sara always becomes upset because I am really a horrible gift receiver. I am a total *beast* at giving gifts, but receiving them? Not so much. She always asks in good time what I want for Christmas or my birthday, but I just never have an answer for her. She really wants to please me, but I never share exactly what I want, so she is left in the dark and has to guess, and I am often halfhearted about what I receive.

I believe we often do the same thing to God. We may spend a lot of time thinking about what we want, but we simply don't verbalize it to Him. If we want to be blessed, we should always find a promise in the Word of God that covers what we're asking for and simply ask for it. In fact, in 1 Thessalonians 5:17, Paul tells us, "Pray without ceasing." This means we should be talking to God morning, noon, and night. That kind of takes the "religion" out of it, though, doesn't it? That ritualistic, formal attitude we feel we need to muster because we only approach God once in a blue moon? No, God is your Father, and Jesus is your best friend; we should pray when we are happy, scared, exhausted, sad, excited, or nervous. If it is the will of God, your prayers will be answered. It won't happen overnight, so don't be discouraged if your prayers aren't immediately answered.

Imagine for a moment, however, what it would be like if God really answered all of our prayers? Think about that for a second. Who would you be married to, what profession would you be in right now, and where you would live? Think about all the prayers you have made—go back to some of the very first ones. If you were anything like me, you made many, many prayer requests, and they flipped and flopped pretty frequently. Can you imagine If God answered all of them? How disastrous would that have been?

You'd probably be married to your first high school crush (can you even imagine?), and you'd probably have become instantly rich and likely have ruined or killed yourself with the money. The truth is that we often pray to accommodate our *flesh's will*, without really considering God's will. James 4:3 says, "You ask and do not receive, because you ask amiss, that you may spend *it* on your pleasures." Contrary to popular belief, we really have no idea what's best for our lives but thankfully, God does.

Proverbs 16:9 says, "A man's heart plans his way, But the Lord directs his steps." I know all too well about making plans and the Lord ultimately disallowing them, but I've learned to trust Him a lot more than I used to. We may be fully convinced the things we desire are best for us, but that's not always true. Does that mean we should stop praying? Of course not! That's the one thing you should do throughout the day, every day. The trouble is that too often we dream more regularly than we pray. Another translation of James 4:3 says we have not because we ask not. I'd like you to really let that sink in. All you really have to do is ask, and if what you're asking for lines up with the Word of God, it's yours. It's really as easy as that, but there are also nuances to this. The Word covers things like healing and provision, but what about the more detailed stuff like what job you should take? Or what you should invest in?

As a child, at a Christian camp program, I learned a song where the chorus went something like, "Don't give up when you pray, God will answer. He hears you. He answers our prayers with exactly what He knows we need. Don't stop praying! He always wants to hear from you." Sometimes, what we are praying for may not be the perfect will of God. I have prayed countless prayers in my life, and I have often begged God to open the doors for my biggest dreams. If I had received everything I had prayed for, I would have been a ship captain, an NFL player, and a coach, all at the same time. Oh, and I'd also be married to Kelly Kapowski from *Saved by the Bell*.

We all have a tendency to pray short-term, halfhearted prayers that we don't really mean because we have only limited sight. Your prayer might be for God to give you a job at a certain company, but God might say no because He has an even better position at a more prestigious company waiting for you. It's hard not to get frustrated, like little children often do, when things don't work out the way we plan them, but God knows what He is doing. It may be hard to understand at the time, but He is in control of every situation we encounter. He knows what is best. For that reason, we must not stop praying and must continue seeking God's will. We need to do it all the time and in all situations. Again, if you are faithful in prayer and study of the Word and if what you desire is in line with God's will (which is found in His Word), it will be answered! Isn't that the best feeling?

I have prayed big and dreamed big, and believe me, God loves dreams. If you are a dreamer, keep dreaming your big dreams. The more your faith grows, the bigger your dreams get; the smaller your dreams, the smaller your faith. As you draw near to Jesus, you will notice your faith, your dreams, and your Godly desires will increase. To be honest, I used to feel like God got in the way of my life. I hated the feeling I had when I was doing something wrong and the gentle but unmistakable voice of the Holy Spirit popped into my heart. What a mood killer.

In hindsight, God was saving and protecting me. He so often prevented me from making mistakes and regrettable choices, often just by causing me to pause and think. It gets more interesting, though; God has also stopped me when I believed I was doing exactly what He wanted me to do. Early on in life, I believed God wanted me to pursue youth ministry at the age of eighteen. I didn't even walk at my high school graduation because I was a youth director at a church, training to become the youth pastor. Being a youth pastor is a good thing, right? I prayed it was God's will to become the youth pastor so I could start my new career. Clear out of the blue, God shut that door, and I thankfully walked away from it. Being a youth pastor may be perfect for someone called to do that, but it was wrong for me.

Later, I wanted to be a football coach. I played football for years, I am a good motivator, and I viewed it as a great opportunity to invest in the lives of young people. Once again, God closed that door. It was very difficult, and I couldn't understand why He would shut doors on such positive opportunities. Years later, it became clear, however, when God opened the door for me to become a Chick-fil-A franchisee. And guess what? I was able to utilize the skills I had learned as a youth pastor and a football coach. As a teenager, when I pictured my future, I never saw myself working with food, but God knew better. In fact, He allowed me to have experiences with guiding, directing, coaching, and organizing people so that I could be a good business owner. He took me through lessons He wanted me to learn in that line of work.

Sometimes God opens doors we aren't interested in, so we shut them and convince ourselves it probably wasn't what God wanted for us. I was truly disappointed when my early dreams were kept from me, but then I realized God had been honing my skills and training me to become a leader the whole time. (Kind of like Mr. Miyagi in *The Karate Kid*—wax on, wax off, right?) Not only that, but with my new position, I was able to pursue ministry because I had a flexible schedule. I learned the very valuable lesson that God is the potter, and I am the clay. He molded and shaped me for just the right time and opportunity, and it could not have worked out any better.

A few years ago, I felt like God was leading me to help a team start a private Christian school. I prayed about it, I put my faith out there, and I felt a calling toward it. Then, I woke up one night and clearly heard God telling me to pull the plug. This was not the calling or plan He had for me. If I have learned anything, it is that we should always be listening for

God because He does speak to us. The problem is that we are not always willing to hear what He has to say because it might not be aligned with what we want. Even though I had been through this lesson before as a young man, I did not want to hear God tell me to abandon my plans to open the school. I felt if I gave it up at that point, it would be embarrassing. I didn't want people to see me as a failure or a quitter, yet I was on the verge of making a huge mistake.

I struggled with this decision for some time, but then I realized an important truth: I would much rather be a failure before men than a failure before God. I don't have to get it perfectly right every time; I only want to follow God's will for my life. I've had to walk away from some dreams, and every single time, I am glad I did. If I had ignored God's voice and pursued opportunities as a coach, youth pastor, or the or joined the board to help start a school, there is no telling how many blessings I would've missed or what kind of messes I would have found myself in. The truth is, I never want to be outside the will of God. Had I gone down any of those paths rather than trust God's leading, I might've married someone else, I might've lived somewhere else, and I might be in a completely different place in my faith than I am now. Pursuing my own dreams is worthless compared to pursuing the dreams God has for me. I am so glad to be on my path with God.

At one point, my wife and I had the opportunity to relocate our Chick-fil-A franchise to Orlando. Moving back to our home state of Florida had been a passion I believe God had put in our hearts, and we were excited to finally get home. However, God shut the door on the Orlando opportunity. When this opportunity presented itself, everything felt right, and we worked hard and pushed ourselves so we could get back to Florida. We tried to make our current restaurant even better so we would be selected for the Florida franchise.

On top of moving back home and receiving a new franchise, there was talk of a second franchise opportunity coming available within a year of us getting the first one! Owning two restaurants instead of one would be incredible (if you own two Chick-fil-A franchises, you are a top dog). The income would have been great, and I would have been better able to provide for my family and give to the Lord. I felt God opened that door for us to be near family, make a comfortable living, start our ministry, and have less to worry about. I excitedly went through the interviews, convincing the selection committee that I was the best candidate, and we prepared ourselves for the move.

We really felt God was in this, but once again, He woke me up in the middle of the night and told me the opportunity was *my* will, not His. He told me the move was not what He was calling us to do, and we needed to stay in California for a while longer. I am so glad God showed me the way, and I'm even more glad I was obedient. Events soon followed that proved we had made the right decision. Had we taken that location in Florida, my mother wouldn't have moved out to California, and my father would not have lost everything. He likely would never have even become a Christian.

As I mentioned earlier in this book, my father wasn't treating my mother the way she deserved to be treated, so she left him and moved to California to get her head together. My mom was the only thing that my dad had left, and when she walked out, his world crumbled, and he ended up on his knees before the Lord. That is when true change finally took place. If we had moved to Florida, perhaps his salvation would have been delayed, and his attitude toward my mom likely wouldn't have changed. I am so thankful I didn't pursue that opportunity, if for no other reason than my father is now a child of the King and will spend eternity in heaven with God. One decision of obedience. That's all it takes. God may redirect your life when you least expect it, and it will always be for a good reason. My dad had a radical change, and God has hold of him and has softened his heart as only the Lord can do (Ezekiel 36:26).

The only way I was able to hear God's voice and be obedient was because I had spent time with Him. You have to spend time with someone to know him or her. We so often try to manufacture perfect lives without input or direction from God, but ironically, the further we are from Him, the more often we must be willing to let doors close. Even when we're close to Him, we get excited about things that are our will, born of the fear and clinging to security we spoke about in the last chapter.

This is one of the aspects of my faith with which I struggle the most. It isn't always easy. We will never know what might have been on the other side of "the door," but God did, and that's really all that matters. When God closes a door, however, He will always open another, better one. He always has a better plan, and He will never just leave us hanging.

Matthew 4:18–20 says,

> And Jesus, walking by the Sea of Galilee, saw two brothers, Simon called Peter, and Andrew his brother, casting a net into the sea; for they were fishermen. Then He said to them, "Follow Me, and I will make you fishers of men." They immediately left *their* nets and followed Him.

I love this verse. Peter and Andrew didn't ask any questions; they simply dropped their nets and followed Jesus. If Jesus spoke to you and wanted to redirect your life, would you be willing to give it all up? If Jesus walked into your home or office and told you to give up everything you have, would you do it? Are you ready to leave your current life for an even better one that God has yet to reveal? We know what Peter or Andrew would have given up if they had been disobedient. And don't believe for a second it wasn't possible; look at Judas.

I believe this chapter explains one of the most critical lessons we can learn when it comes to the call of God. It is a lesson for those who are really maturing as believers, so I encourage you to let it sink in. You know the voice of God when He speaks. We all reason it "might be our head," but weigh up any decisions with the Word, and if God says go— then go! If He says no, and you still go, then you will be out of His will and largely out from under His perfect covering. Instead, allow Him to lead you. I promise you, He has only the very best for you in mind, as we will see clearly in the next chapter.

22

Heaven Focused

One of my favorite movies is *Wall Street: Money Never Sleeps*. The main character, Gordon Gekko, is a sadistic fiend driven by his adoration of money. Gordon is so greedy that in the movie he says, "Someone reminded me I once said 'Greed is good.' Now it seems it's legal because everyone is drinking the same Kool-Aid." Yes, there are people like this, and it shows where Gordon's heart and mind are focused. It also shows where the world has been headed for some time now.

Another movie I enjoy is *Up in the Air*, with George Clooney. You can't go wrong with a Clooney flick and honestly, I am a huge fan of his acting. In the movie, Clooney's character, Ryan, is a "corporate downsizer" who flies all around the world to terminate people's jobs as efficiently as possible. Through his work, Ryan develops a granite exterior and works hard at allowing zero emotional attachment to the people he is letting go. The logic is that will be a much less painful encounter for all involved.

Ryan does so much flying in all his firing that he is one of those people you'd be lucky to be behind at security in the airport; he travels light, his shoes are off, and there is never anything in his pockets. This guy knows the drill and doesn't mess around. The focus of the story, however, is Ryan's sky miles; he travels so much he is determined to earn a rare black rewards card for having traveled ten million miles. In the movie, this is something only six other people have ever done.

One of the masterful innuendos of the commentary is that Ryan never redeems any of his sky miles so he can eventually obtain this prestigious card, which will be hand-delivered by a captain. Through various twists and turns, and at the obvious price of what is left of his humanity, Ryan ultimately reaches his goal. On his next flight, the captain approaches him with much ado and presents to him the sacred black card. The captain also tells Ryan he is the youngest person ever to have achieved this milestone. Then he asks where Ryan is from. Ryan ponders this for a moment and then answers he is from "here." The captain is puzzled at first, but Ryan explains he is from wherever they are at any given moment.

He has been so focused on his sky miles that he no longer has any place to call home. In the narrative, Ryan explains he spent so much of his life traveling and striving to earn this black card that he had no permanent place to rest his head. He is suddenly baffled by the pointlessness of it all.

I see several parallels between Ryan's predicament and my own life. There are things I've saved up for or spent a good deal of time trying to achieve, but in the end, they always turn out to be a near-complete waste of time, energy, and money. It reminds me of Luke 12:13–21, where Jesus shares the following:

> Then one from the crowd said to Him, "Teacher, tell my brother to divide the inheritance with me."

> But He said to him, "Man, who made Me a judge or an arbitrator over you?" And He said to them, "Take heed and beware of covetousness, for one's life does not consist in the abundance of the things he possesses."

> Then He spoke a parable to them, saying: "The ground of a certain rich man yielded plentifully. And he thought within himself, saying, 'What shall I do, since I have no room to store my crops?' So he said, 'I will do this: I will pull down my barns and build greater, and there I will store all my crops and my goods. And I will say to my soul, "Soul, you have many goods laid up for many years; take your ease; eat, drink, and be merry."' But God said to him, 'Fool! This night your soul will be

required of you; then whose will those things be which you have provided?' So *is* he who lays up treasure for himself, and is not rich toward God."

If Jesus looked at my life, what would He see? What am I working toward, and what am I storing up? Do I spend my extra time and energy working toward a classic car I've had my eye on, a designer jacket, or money in my portfolio so I am prepared for retirement? What does that even mean? Can I buy another home, sit on the beach, go out to dinner every night, and take exotic vacations? More importantly, is that really what God wants me to do?

If my life were truly demanded from me tonight, or when I am fifty, or when I retire at sixty-five, what worldly possessions would I have stowed away for safekeeping? I guarantee the first thing my wife will do is burn my collection of football trading cards. What would have been the point of spending money on them, never taking them out of the package, and hoping they accumulate wealth someday? It becomes silly when you really take a look at your life like that.

When I thought about this, I discovered that especially earlier in life, I was usually storing up for *myself*. It goes beyond material possessions as well; even in my daily business, I try to store up energy, emotions, money, and time. I try to calculate how much of each of these things should be spent on certain things throughout the day. If you were to evaluate your life, what treasures are you storing up on earth? Maybe it's not frequent flyer miles (or maybe it is). Maybe it's the cars in your garage, your house itself, or the important people with which you surround yourself. I'll bet there is always something—it's part of our flawed human nature. Sometimes, I'm ashamed to admit I even store up favors. I know if I do something nice for someone, they'll feel obliged to return the favor. In time, I'll get something I need from them.

In contrast, how much do we really focus on storing up treasures in heaven? Have you ever thought about what that means? When we "store up treasures in heaven," it means we have a heaven-focused mind-set rather than focusing on the accumulation of earthly goods. In Luke 15:7, Jesus says, "I say to you that likewise there will be more joy in heaven over one sinner who repents than over ninety-nine just persons who need no repentance." Clearly, the most valuable prize to the Lord is a saved soul, yet we are obsessed with our 401(k)s.

You should know by now I'm *not saying* don't save for retirement or that making money or having nice things is bad. If, however, these things replace our primary focus of the calling we have in service to the Lord, I'll readily shout they are bad from the rooftops. Again, as expressed in other chapters but worth reiterating here, it comes down to focus. If we focus on the Lord and the things that bring Him joy, such as serving and giving and reaching the lost, we will automatically spend less time focusing on our own selfish desires.

In Matthew 6:21, Jesus said, "Where your treasure is, so will your heart be also." Your treasure is whatever you spend your time thinking about the most, trying to obtain, obsessing over, and wasting money on. Letting go of my concerns over worldly treasures gives me a chance to fully rely on God and trust that He will provide for my needs. What is your treasure?

Sometimes I feel sad living in California because I see people overextend themselves by purchasing extravagances they don't need and can't afford just to keep up appearances. I wish I could tell these people I have been in their shoes and have learned it doesn't matter what anyone thinks of the home you have, the car you drive, or the clothes you wear. What matters to God is what is in your *heart*. What matters to God is what you do with what He has given you. What matters to God is that you are rich in heaven and rich in His calling on your life.

As we approach the end of this book, I wanted to write this short chapter as a reminder to consider putting your calling above all else. It is also good to remember our lives could be required at any time and we are to work with an urgency. I might not see the end of this day, and you might not get to finish this book. But also think about the beauty of storing heavenly treasures; not only will your rewards will never fade, lose their value, or go out of style, but souls will be rescued from the devil's clutches. In movies, we see the quote "I owe you my life" all the time. Imagine saving someone's *eternal life*. Focusing on eternal ends means you will be far more satisfied and receive far more joy, so without a doubt, a heavenly perspective is a complete win-win.

But, friend, although there is so much joy when we find our purpose, there is also much urgency. Do you think the distractions I have mentioned in this chapter are accidental? Do you think your enemy just leaves you alone and leaves you to maybe accept your calling or maybe pursue temporal things? No, he has a plan for your life as much as God does. Think about that too. You may have to work a little to identify your calling, if you haven't already, and you will definitely have to work to remain focused on it through trusting your Savior.

If you still haven't identified your calling or you are still unsure about how to store up riches in heaven, the last chapter is just for you. Let's take a look and see if you can find what will get you moving to your eternal destiny.

23

You're on Deck

As we embark on the final chapter of this book, I hope you know my goal isn't to scare you, put undue pressure on you, or make you feel guilty. Rather, the single goal of my stories and testimony is to inspire you to go out into the world and find the joy waiting for you that you could never imagine unless you take some active steps. Yes, sometimes it is good if someone holds up a mirror and allows us to ask some difficult questions, so even though I have done this at times in this book, my goal has only been to encourage, motivate, and excite you. Because it really is an exciting adventure that awaits you.

In this last chapter, I want to emphasize the *urgency* of our calling. Please note, I do not want to induce anxiety, as that is never God's plan (Philippians 4:6), but I do want you to take action toward your calling. Especially in the uncertain times we live in, it's always important to remember today is a gift. We never really know when our time is up. God promises He will satisfy us with long life (Psalm 91:16), and that is a promise we can rest in. However, some of us are called to leave this earth early for some reason, and sometimes things happen we certainly don't understand. Although I know there is a sound reason for everything that happens, we should never take tomorrow for granted. The Apostle James even tell us:

> Whereas you do not know what *will happen* tomorrow. For what is your life? It is even a vapor that appears for a little time and then vanishes away. (James 4:14)

God tells us in many places in the Word that our days are numbered; clearly, it is appointed for every single one of us to leave this earth at some point. It's a balancing act we learn, however, and we have to make smart choices but should still live today to the fullest. You can't know when your last day may come, and that should instill some urgency in you to share the gospel. This is our mission in life. As I share the following three stories, I hope you will consider what these people had and the importance of their lives.

I am writing the first draft of this chapter the day after Paul Walker died. Paul is the renowned actor from the *Fast and the Furious* franchise (and many more films), who passed away in a terrible car accident. I live near the site of the accident, which could be why his death hit me so hard. Maybe Paul's death saddened me more than most because I loved the *Fast and the Furious* movies, or maybe it was because I had heard about what a good guy he was, or perhaps it just reminded me of the brevity of life. Paul was only forty when he died and left behind a teenage daughter. He was a passenger in his friend's Porsche GT when the driver lost control of the car; it crashed into a tree, ripped in half, and burst into flames. The wreck was so horrific that the two men had to be identified by their dental records.

Paul Walker's death was difficult to comprehend, in part because he seemed like such a genuinely good guy. In the wake of the tragedy, the media shared behind-the-scenes stories of his life and how he genuinely did many good deeds for many people. Despite being an "A-list" Hollywood star, Paul was a kind and generous soul who remained very close to his family. The primary buzz of the Internet, however, was where all of his money would go. Paul had a net worth of $45 million, and that's mostly what people cared about. Of course, as a follower of Jesus Christ, my primary question was whether he was saved. I wondered if anyone ever truly shared God's love with him and if he had accepted Christ as his Lord. I pray with all my heart that someone did.

The next story I'd like to share is about Lee Roy Selmon, an NFL star who played with the Tampa Bay Buccaneers. Lee Roy was so talented that he was drafted in the first round and ultimately was crowned a Hall of Fame defensive end. Lee Roy was a strong Christian with great morals and a passionate heart for people. With his football fortune, he developed a chain of restaurants, named simply Lee Roy Selmon's, that serves all the southern foods his mom used to cook when he was growing up. (If you ever get a chance to visit one, get the Twisted Chicken; it's life changing.)

Sadly, at only fifty-six years old, Lee Roy passed away from a stroke; he seemed to have a lot of life ahead of him. Many people were interviewed after his untimely death, including former teammates and family, and every one of them spoke of the caliber of his character and the high quality of man he was. Surprisingly, his exceptional football talents were barely mentioned, despite his many accomplishments on the field. This was because the positivity and light in his life outshone even what he achieved as a hall-of-famer. I believe the light of Christ in Lee Roy's life was how he was able to use his fame after football in such a positive way.

I was blessed enough to meet Lee Roy when he visited a football camp I hosted for inner-city youth. I invited him, figuring the worst he could do was say no, but he said yes, and he actually came! Lee Roy played football with the kids, taught them some plays, and shared his relationship with Jesus. It was a beautiful day, and to me, that was his true legacy.

My last story is about a family friend named Fred, who owned the wedding company where my mother worked for many years. Fred started each morning with a large pile of vitamins and supplements, lived a very healthy life, and was in great shape. One morning, while at home getting ready to perform a wedding ceremony, Fred had a sudden and massive heart attack. He died that day. Fred was not a Christian, he did not have a relationship with Jesus that I knew of, and unfortunately, by all indications, he will not spend eternity with his Creator.

I want you to notice that each of these men was blessed with wealth. Paul Walker was a movie star, Lee Roy Selmon was a professional athlete, and Fred was a successful small business owner. What do they have in common? They all left things behind. They had dreams, ambitions, money, cars, houses, and families, but in the end, none of that mattered. All of their material possessions were left to be divided up among their families. Sure, it is good to leave an inheritance to your children, but after that, who really cares in the end? Those are just material items. I have peace knowing Lee Roy was a Christian and is in heaven with his Savior. I pray that Paul and Fred knew the Lord before they passed away.

So as we close this chapter and this book, I want to ask you to take some time to evaluate your life. What are you focused on? I'm almost certain Paul Walker had no idea the day of that crash would be his last. Lee Roy Selmon had no idea he would have a stroke and die young. Fred died unexpectedly in his bathroom, with other plans for his day and what he thought would be the rest of his life. Our days are numbered. We don't know when our time is up. These are not concerns for us to trouble ourselves with, though; God has it all under His control. But ask yourself if you are prepared to die. Are you treating today like the gift it is? Are you prepared to give an account of your talents to your Creator?

Tim McGraw wrote a song that seems especially appropriate here. He sang,

> I went skydiving, I went Rocky Mountain climbing, I went 2.7 seconds on a bull named Fu Manchu. And I loved deeper, and I spoke sweeter, and I gave forgiveness I've been denying. Someday I hope you get the chance to live like you were dying.[1]

I know I don't always live like that. I don't always forgive quickly. I don't always push myself out of my comfort zone. I don't always love recklessly. I don't always share my faith with those who need it. What about you? Do you live like you are dying? Because think about it…that is exactly what is happening. What is the purpose of this life if we don't share Jesus?

In his song, McGraw continued,

> I was finally the husband that most of the time I wasn't, and I became the friend a friend would like to have. And all of a sudden, going fishing wasn't such an imposition, and I went three times that year I lost my dad. I finally read the Good Book, and I took a good, long, hard look at what I'd do if I could do it all again… like tomorrow was a gift, and you've got eternity to think about what you'd do with it. What could you do with it? What would I do with it?

1. Tim McGraw. "Live like You Were Dying." Curb Records, 2004, audio CD.

Isn't that powerful? The message there, I believe, is that we won't get a do-over in life. Make it count and live it fully. Are you wasting your days dreaming about things that won't matter in the end? Or are you impacting lives for eternity? Are you making a difference? Are you living life with the knowledge that there are true riches in heaven that surpass anything in this lifetime? As you finish this book, I ask you to pray and find out what God wants for you. Then watch and see what doors of opportunity He opens for you. Because I assure you, God will open them.

In Mark 16:15, Jesus says, "Go into all the world and preach the gospel to every creature." So just go! Close this book, get off your behind, and do it! Don't wait a second longer. Call that friend or family member you have been avoiding, reach out to that hurting person at work, and utilize every single opportunity God sets before you. The time is now and truly, we don't have anything except that.

Preach the gospel in word and deed, for we never know what today holds.

May God bless you more than you ever dreamed as you obey Him.

Made in the USA
Charleston, SC
22 May 2016